THE BEER
COMPANION

THE BEER COMPANION

AN ESSENTIAL GUIDE TO CLASSIC BEERS FROM AROUND THE WORLD

—BRIAN GLOVER—

LORENZ BOOKS

First published in 1999 by Lorenz Books

© Anness Publishing Limited 1999

Lorenz Books is an imprint of
Anness Publishing Limited
Hermes House
88–89 Blackfriars Road
London SE1 8HA

Published in the USA by Lorenz Books, Anness Publishing Inc.,
27 West 20th Street, New York, NY 10011; (800) 354 9657

This edition distributed in Canada by Raincoast Books, 8680 Cambie Street,
Vancouver, British Columbia, V6P 6M9

ISBN 0 7548 0173 X

A CIP catalogue record for this book is available from the British Library

Publisher: Joanna Lorenz
Project Editor: Zoe Antoniou
Designer: Kathryn Gammon
Photographers: William Lingwood and David Jordan
Jacket Photographer: William Lingwood
Stylist: Clare Louise Hunt
Editorial Reader: Diane Ashmore
Production Controller: Joanna King

The publishers would like to thank the following: Brian Glover for his kind assistance and for supplying beer mats and labels, The Beer Shop,
14 Pitfield Street, London N1 6HA for supplying beer for photography, and breweries who supplied images: Pyramid Breweries Inc. (p25tl),
Marston's (p28t), Young's (pp28bl+br, 29bl+t, 30t, 31bl) and Bass (p32bl).
Picture credits: The Advertising Archives (pp3, 5, 16br, 27br, 33 centre, 48bl), e t archive (pp8t, 8bl, 11t, 24bl), Hulton Getty (pp9t, 10br, 23t, 26t,
26br, 27bl, 32t, 61b), Kobal (p12t) and Tony Stone (pp12b, 20t, 22br, 26bl, 27t, 31tl, 34t, 55t). (r=right, l=left, t=top, b=bottom).

Printed and bound in Singapore

1 3 5 7 9 10 8 6 4 2

Contents

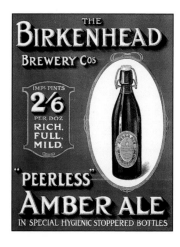

Introduction

Beer has always been known as the drink of the people. While malt and hops may not have inspired as many noble writings as the elite grape, they are important ingredients in this best and most sociable of long drinks that is enjoyed around the world. Beer is an ancient drink with a fascinating and varied history, and so there are many stories to be told about this classic brew.

Beer, one of the world's most satisfying of drinks, has played a very important role in many of the major cultures of the past, although its origins have now been lost in the mists of time. It has been used by preachers as a religious symbol, by doctors as a medicinal treatment and by workers as a means of relaxation after a hard day's toil. Throughout the ages, in different countries, beer has been promoted as a health concoction as well as reviled as the drink of the devil.

In the mid-19th century, archaeologists excavating Egyptian tombs came across remnants of baskets full of grain that had been preserved for centuries among treasures. Evidence here suggests that beer as well as bread would accompany an Egyptian king on his travels into the next world. By the Middle Ages, brewing was taking place within monasteries, and today, famous Trappist beers are still brewed in Belgium and Holland. In medieval times, "ale wives" were brewing in their kitchens and the popularity of beer was becoming established in growing towns and cities, where it was often safer to drink than polluted water.

The brewing process has now changed in a fundamental way since these early times, and has developed into one of the largest and most modern multinational industries. Beer itself has been affected profoundly by advances in technology since the Industrial Revolution of the 19th century. Many giant breweries now labour to produce beers with the widest possible acceptance level and, inevitably, the least possible character. However, demand for specialist quality beers, particularly in recent years, has meant that there is still room for smaller-scale producers in today's richly varied marketplace, and many small and micro-breweries have grown up all over the world.

The huge range of beers is dazzling, as is the variety of customs associated with it. From fruit beers to Pilsners, from porters to "real ale", the choice has never been greater. This book explores the story of beer and which glasses to raise at the global bar.

ABOVE: The varying hues of a bitter, a fruit beer and a lager.

OPPOSITE: A long glass of stout, Pilsner or bitter, enjoyed in a relaxing, social setting, is an immensely satisfying drink.

A Long Tradition

It is not known exactly when or where the first brewing took place. Existing records show how the early Middle Eastern civilizations had developed it to a fine art, and that beer was evident in ancient Egypt. However, grain-based alcohol was being made long before either of these cultures were brewing beer, and it developed independently more or less the world over – the end product depending on what local crops and fruits were available at the time.

The Africans were making some of the first intoxicating drinks using sorghum and millet, and Brazilian Indians were known to produce dark, smoky-tasting brews from manioc roots and grain roasted over hardwood fires. South American Indian women brewed *chicha*, which is still made in some countries today, by chewing maize kernels, spitting them into pots and leaving them to ferment.

The discovery of the remains of a brewery in western Texas in 1938, revealed that the early North Americans were also brewing, and it is known that the Aztecs in Mexico had their own beer gods.

ABOVE: An ancient-Egyptian female kneading dough to make beer, in the fifth dynasty.

LEFT: An Aztec woman serves maguey root beer.

Meanwhile, the Chinese were brewing rice and millet at the same time as the ancient Egyptians, but using much more advanced techniques.

THE ANCIENT WORLD

The first detailed mention of beer was made more than 5,000 years ago by the Sumerians, who lived in the area now known as Iraq. Among surviving clay tablets, more than 20 varieties of beer are mentioned, as well as many recipes that included beer as an ingredient. One type of beer made from liquid bread, called *sikaru*, played a symbolic role in Sumerian culture.

Early brewing was a domestic activity and did not require any special buildings or equipment. A combined maltings, bakery and brewhouse consisted of a mud or reed hut with an oven, a mat and a few earthen vessels. Two flat stones served as a mill. Later, as the civilizations of the Middle

8

East became more sophisticated, larger brewing operations met the needs of the army, temples and palaces. Excavations at Ur have uncovered a brewery dating from between 2000 and 539 BC.

From as early as 3000 BC, the Egyptians were brewing a strong beer flavoured with juniper, ginger, saffron and herbs, called *heget*, also known by its Greek name, *zythum*. An ancient papyrus gives instructions for brewing *zythum*, a stronger beer called *dizythum* and a weak family beer, *busa*. The Egyptian "Book of the Dead" contains a reference to an offering of *zythum* at the altar, and Osiris, one of Egypt's most important gods, was believed to be the protector of brewers.

Later on, the art of brewing on a grand scale was perfected, and the Egyptians also developed the malting process that had been discovered earlier in Mesopotamia, which was the practice of part-baking cereal grains.

By the 8th century AD, Egypt had been invaded by Muslims, whose holy book, the Koran, bans the drinking of alcohol. The

ABOVE RIGHT: A cartoon illustrates a domestic home-brewing scene.

RIGHT: Fraoch, or "heather ale", is one of many recent beers that revives the ancient art of brewing.

BELOW: A selection of bottled beers from around the world.

Egyptian brewing industry went into a decline from which it never recovered. However, the knowledge of beer-making had already spread. In the 1st century AD, the Roman historian Tacitus stated that beer was the usual drink of the Germans, Gauls and the Norsemen of the far north. The drink began to further establish itself as it followed the route of the cultivation of grain to Europe, while wine dominated the warmer regions of the Mediterranean where the vine reigned supreme.

A MEDIEVAL TALE

In medieval times, beer became very popular. It was considered as more than a warming and intoxicating refreshment as it also provided a safe drink when the purity of water and milk was uncertain and drinks such as tea and coffee were unknown. The process of boiling, followed by the production of alcohol, removed the main dangers of any infection. In Britain, beer was commonly brewed at home by women who were known as "ale wives".

The everyday drink was weak beer, while stronger beers were used for special occasions. Brewers used many cereals, including wheat, rye and oats, but increasingly barley was preferred because it was easier to malt and produced more sugar, which then turned to alcohol. Herbs and spices were often used to flavour stronger beers.

THE HOLY ALLIANCE

Monks throughout Europe helped to nurture the art of brewing. Large-scale breweries could be found in the monastic settlements that sprung up across Europe from the 5th century onwards. They satisfied not only their own needs, but also those of thirsty travellers and pilgrims. Many monks secured their financial stability through the sale of ale outside the walls.

Holy communities in Central Europe are credited with being the first to brew with hops. This crop was introduced not so much for its flavour – many drinkers did not welcome the bitter taste – but for its preservative value. Monasteries were so central to the development of brewing in England that the industry even adopted the monks' method of marking the strength of beer, with crosses on the barrels.

LAGER ARRIVES

The monks of Bavaria were responsible for discovering a new innovation – bottom-fermentation. In the hot summer months, fermentation could run out of control and spoil the brew. When Bavarian monasteries stored beer for long periods in cool cellars, they found that the yeasts sank to the bottom of the vessel instead of frothing at the top, and so fermented more slowly. This bottom-fermented beer could be stored for much longer periods, and became known as "lagering", from the German word for storage.

ABOVE: St Paul Abbey beers imitate surviving Belgian beers.

LEFT: Lager has now become one of the most widely drunk beers.

RIGHT: Traditional wooden barrels for transporting beer have now largely disappeared.

ROLL OUT THE BARREL

As the Industrial Revolution swept across Europe from the 18th century, new innovations and discoveries coupled with new demands from the industrial workers transformed the local craft of brewing into a much larger industry. As a result, how to effectively transport the hefty beer barrels became a key issue.

Many larger, commercial breweries were established alongside rivers, to allow boats to transport beer further afield, but poor roads and the relatively low value of beer meant that it was not worthwhile to transport it any distance. The development of firstly a canal system, and then the railways and steam-powered machinery soon changed everything. Large casks of beer could be transported easily, inexpensively and relatively rapidly, and the era of the national brewing companies began.

The breweries were quick to take advantage of scientific innovations, such as thermometers and hydrometers. Many of the most famous British and Irish breweries date from this period – William Younger of Edinburgh (1749), Arthur Guinness of Dublin (1759) and William Bass of Burton (1777). In 1796, the Whitbread brewery in London produced a record 200,000 barrels in one year.

As the beer industry grew, refrigeration became a key issue as transport had been. The need to control temperature as part of the storing process as well as the demand by drinkers for an ice-cold thirst-quenching draught (draft) made refrigeration essential. Initially, improved transport allowed greater use of ice from lakes and mountains. However, with the development of a compression machine in the 1850s by James Harrison of Geelong, Australia, mechanical refrigeration had effectively arrived and breweries were quick to install them. By the late 1870s, Anheuser-Busch introduced the first fleet of refrigerated railway freight wagons.

☆ PURE GOLD ☆

On 5 October, 1842, the Bavarian brewer Josef Groll mashed a batch of beer in the Bohemian town of Plzen, and the world's first ever golden-coloured lager was born. Until then, lagered beers were a dark brown or amber-red colour. This development was possibly an accident, resulting from locally grown barley that was low in protein and local water containing limestone, which tends to draw colour from the malt.

At the time, the town was known by its German name of Pilsen. The Pilsner style was soon copied across the world. Pils or Pilsner-inspired lagers are now the most widely brewed international beer.

THE DEMON DRINK

The growing ranks of industrial workers, who despite appalling conditions in the factories were still more affluent than their country cousins, found comfort in cheap and powerful beer. As a result, public bars rapidly appeared in the cities.

Religious leaders soon became appalled by the spreading social evil of drunkenness. The church was particularly keen to outlaw drinking on the Sabbath. Scotland, despite a thriving brewing industry in Edinburgh, Glasgow and Alloa, took the first step and forced through the Forbes Mackenzie Act in 1853, which introduced the Sunday closing of pubs. In 1878, the Irish followed and, in 1881, Wales obtained its own Sunday Closing Act.

During World War I, the Defence of the Realm Act of 1915 reduced the number of opening hours for British pubs. Lloyd George, the Prime Minister in 1916, claimed that, "Drink is doing

ABOVE: *"Canvassing for Votes", by the painter William Hogarth, depicts a street scene outside an English tavern.*

11

us more damage in the war than all of the German submarines put together". Some countries did not shrink from a total ban on alcohol. Canada introduced national Prohibition in 1918. New Zealand, Australia and other European countries teetered on the brink, and many nations, while not banning alcohol entirely, restricted the sale of spirits, including beer-loving Belgium.

However, the British government took a different view towards beer by World War II, when it was seen as vital for maintaining morale. "Make sure that the beer – four pints a week – goes to the troops under fire before any of the parties in the rear get a drop," thundered Prime Minister Winston Churchill.

ABOVE: Harry Andrews, Anthony Quayle, Sylvia Sims and John Mills enjoy a glass of beer in the feature film, "Ice Cold in Alex".

RIGHT: A man in traditional dress enjoys a drink at the famous Bavarian beer festival Oktoberfest, held in Munich, Germany.

ABOVE RIGHT: Bottled beers and beer mats from around the world.

FAR RIGHT: Cans of beer, from Foster's, Budweiser and Holsten.

THE UNITED STATES

By the second half of the 19th century, thousands of breweries from New York to Milwaukee were producing a wide spectrum of beers, from Pilsners to porters. In 1890, Philadelphia alone boasted 94 breweries. However, the flood of immigrants, many extremely poor, also brought widespread social problems. Drunkenness was one of them and temperance campaigners began to find converts. In 1826, Reverend Lyman Beecher founded the American Temperance Union, which initially objected only to strong spirits, but ten years later opposed all intoxicants.

In 1833, the Supreme Court ruled that each state was free to regulate the liquor trade within its own borders and by 1919, 27 states had adopted Prohibition. The First Lady, Mrs Rutherford B. Hayes, banned drink at the White House and was christened "Lemonade Lucy" by her husband's political opponents.

The 65th United States Congress of 1917 was dedicated to putting the nation on a war footing against Germany, and some rulings were set up to ban the manufacture and sale of alcohol, which were reinforced in 1919 with the National Prohibition Act.

Not only were the laws widely evaded, but Prohibition encouraged a new criminal culture built around smuggling and selling hard liquor and beer, which was tacitly supported by a large sec-

tion of the population. New York, which had 15,000 bars before Prohibition, soon concealed an estimated 32,000 undercover drinking dens, or, "speakeasies". Prohibition was causing a complete breakdown in law and order, and public opinion turned against it. When Franklin D. Roosevelt pledged to repeal the 18th Amendment in 1932, he was duly elected President.

INTERNATIONAL GROWTH

In the years following the repeal of Prohibition, a small number of giant companies came to dominate the revived American brewing industry. In countries where Prohibition had not laid its withering hand on the brewing business, the same process of concentration was taking place, but at a slower pace. France had boasted 3,543 breweries in 1905, but 90 years later, fewer than 20 remained.

In Britain, the Canadian Eddie Taylor introduced the lager Carling Black Label into Britain by buying 12 breweries to form Northern United Breweries. In the 1960s, six large groups controlled the bulk of the beer trade, becoming three by 1997. Just over 50 surviving regional breweries were left with around 15 per cent of the market. In France, BSN (Kronenbourg) and Heineken,

 now account for three-quarters of the market and in Denmark, Carlsberg controls that amount itself. In Australia, Foster's and Lion Nathan control 90 per cent of the trade and in Canada, Molson and Labatt are similar.

☆ THE CONSUMER STRIKES BACK ☆

In 1971, a handful of British drinkers, led by journalists Michael Hardman and Graham Lees formed the Campaign for Real Ale – CAMRA. Their aim was to promote real living ale that continues to ferment and develop its full flavour in the cask. This movement was in direct response to the carbonated and pasteurized keg beers that were dominating British pubs, such as Watney's Red.

Regional breweries welcomed the new strident voice of the consumer and others began to put hand-pumps back on the bar to serve cask beer. CAMRA was extremely successful. Interest in traditional beers has caught on throughout the world. The European Beer Consumers Union helps to preserve a European beer culture, and in the United States, the arrival of small and micro-breweries has been very successful. The total number of new breweries has grown to over 1,000 in the United States today.

Not all countries have rushed headlong down this narrowing path. In Germany, many smaller breweries have survived, helped by the loyalty of the conservative German drinker. However, falling demand has meant that these are beginning to disappear too.

Brewing is no longer a national but an international industry. Some breweries have sold beer beyond their borders for decades, even centuries, such as the Dublin-based giant Guinness and the German breweries Beck's, St Pauli Girl and Löwenbräu. Others have established licensing agreements to have their beers brewed abroad by local breweries. Leading beer brands are now well known across the world.

The Types of Beer

There is a rich variety of beer tastes to explore around the world. There are roughly two main beer categories, namely ale (or, top-fermented beer) and lager (bottom-fermented). The range of different styles within these general terms is immense, from dark, hearty ales to tangy, spritzy gueuzes. The myriad contrasting tastes, colours, flavours and aromas can, to some extent, be squeezed into the following smaller groupings with similar characteristics and methods of production.

ABBEY BEERS

Strong, fruity ales, abbey beers are brewed in Belgium, sometimes under licence from religious communities. They copy the style of the surviving beers produced in monasteries, and usually name their brews after a church or saint.

ALT

Alt (*above*) means "traditional" or "old" in German, and Altbier indicates a bitter-tasting brew produced by an ancient style of brewing using top-fermentation. Alt is a copper-coloured aromatic ale, containing just over 4.5% alcohol. It is made in Düsseldorf and a few other cities in northern Germany.

BARLEY WINE

Barley wine is the English name for a powerful, almost syrupy strong ale that is usually sold in small, nip-size bottles. These well-matured brews can be golden or dark in colour. The darker versions were once called "Stingo".

BERLINER WEISSE

A light, sharply acidic German wheat beer made mainly in Berlin, this refreshing brew is relatively low in alcohol. It has a cloudy white (*weisse*) appearance and is often laced with a dash of green woodruff or raspberry juice to add colour.

BIÈRE DE GARDE

A top-fermenting "beer for keeping" from north-west France, it is a medium to strong spicy ale. Some of these are bottle-conditioned and many are sealed with champagne-style wired corks.

BITTER

This distinctive dry and hoppy type of draught (draft) ale (*below*) in England and Wales is traditionally reddish amber in colour, although paler varieties are now popular. Alcohol content is usually 3–5%, but stronger versions exist, often called Best or Special.

BLACK BEER

Schwarzbier is a strong-tasting, bitter-chocolate lager, a speciality of eastern Germany. It is also made in Japan.

In England, especially Yorkshire, black beers are strong, pitch-black, treacly malt extracts, usually bottled for mixing with lemonade (lemon soda) to make distinctive shandies.

BOCK

This strong, malty, warming German beer of about 6.5% alcohol was traditionally dark in colour and is now more likely to be golden bronze. This powerful, smooth brew originated in Einbeck in Lower Saxony, but is now brewed in other countries. Doppelbocks, and particularly Eisbocks, are stronger versions.

BROWN ALE

Once a popular English working man's drink, this sweetish, bottled mild ale is dark in colour and low in alcohol. The north-east of the country produces stronger, drier versions. Sweet-and-sour ones are produced in East Flanders in Belgium.

CHILLI BEER

Produced by only a handful of American breweries, this is an odd, slow-burning speciality that is said to go well with Mexican food.

CREAM ALE

A sweetish, smooth, golden ale from the United States, it was originally introduced by ale brewers trying to copy the Pilsner style.

DIÄT PILS

This lager undergoes a thorough fermentation, which removes nearly all the sugars from the bottom-fermented, Pilsner-derived brew. A strong, dry-tasting beer, it is still packed with calories in the alcohol. It was originally brewed as a beer suitable for diabetics, rather than slimmers (dieters), but its name misled many and the word diät has now been removed.

DORTMUNDER

This strong, malty, dry, full-bodied lager is from Dortmund, the biggest brewing city in Europe. Originally brewed for export, it was once sold across the globe. Its alcohol content is 5.5%.

DRY BEER

First produced in Japan by the Asahi Brewery in 1987, this is a super diät Pils with a parching effect and little taste, which was initially widely adopted in North America.

DUNKEL

German lagers were traditionally dark. Dunkels (*left*) from Bavaria are soft, malty, brown beers with 4.5% alcohol.

FARO

Once the most common manifestation of Belgian lambic beer, this sweetened version has now largely disappeared.

FRAMBOISE/FRAMBOZEN

These are the French and Flemish names for a Belgian fruit beer, which is made by adding raspberries to a lambic. This has a sparkling, pink champagne character with a light, fruity flavour. Other fruits have been tried with varying degrees of success.

GREEN BEER

Green beer (*right*) is young beer that has not had time to mature. The term also denotes a beer made with organically grown malt and hops, known as *biologique* in France and *biologisch* in Germany.

GUEUZE

Young and old lambics are blended, triggering a secondary fermentation that results in a distinctive sparkling beer with a fruity, sour, dry taste.

HEFE

Hefe (*right*) is German for "yeast", and this describes an unfiltered beer with a sediment in the bottle. Draught (draft) beers, "mit Hefe", are usually cloudy.

HELL

Meaning "pale" or "light", hell indicates a mild, malty, golden lager, which is often from Munich.

HONEY BEER

A few English breweries have revived an old tradition of producing a honey brew. Some new American brewers also use honey, as do the innovative Belgian De Dolle Brouwers in their Boskeun beer.

ICE BEER

Ice beer (*below*) is a style in which the beer is frozen after fermentation, giving a cleaner, almost smoothed-away flavour. It was originally developed in Canada by Labatt. Sometimes the ice crystals are removed to increase the strength of the beer. Most major United States brewers have launched their own brands, such as Bud Ice.

IPA

India Pale Ale (*right*) is a strong, heavily hopped beer, originally brewed in Britain to withstand long sea voyages to distant parts of the British Empire. Specialist American brewers now probably produce the most authentic versions.

IRISH ALE

This soft, slightly sweet, reddish ale is produced commercially, but Smithwick's of Kilkenny is the best-known in Ireland today.

KÖLSCH

This light, subtle, fruity-tasting beer, with 4–5 % alcohol, is a top-fermenting ale, although it resembles Pilsner in appearance. It is produced in Cologne.

KRIEK

In this Belgian lambic beer, secondary fermentation is stimulated with cherries for a dry, fruity flavour.

KRISTALL

This German term, meaning "crystal-clear", usually indicates a filtered wheat beer or Weizenbier.

LIGHT ALE

In England, this indicates a bottled, low-gravity bitter. In Scotland, it means the weakest brew.

LITE

In North America, this denotes a thin, low-calorie beer, with Miller Lite, Coors Light and Bud Light being the best known. In Australia and some other countries, it indicates low-alcohol beer.

LOW ALCOHOL

Since the late 1980s, many breweries have added low-alcohol (up to 2.5%) or no-alcohol (less than 0.05%) beers to their range, mainly in response to increasingly strict drink-driving laws. Some of these near beers are produced by using yeasts that create little alcohol and sometimes fermentation is cut short. In others, the alcohol is removed from normal beer.

☆ LAMBIC BEER ☆

One of the most primitive beers brewed on earth, these spontaneously fermenting beers are unique to an area to the west of Brussels, in the Senne Valley of Belgium. Lambic brewers use at least 30 per cent unmalted wheat in order to produce a milky wort from the mash. Old hops are used as they are required only for their preservative value, not for flavour or aroma.

The wheat brew is left exposed to the air to allow spontaneous fermentation, and is only brewed in the cooler months of the year. The fermenting wort is then run into large wooden casks and left to ferment for many years.

It is a unique, tart sour beer with a taste almost like a flat acidic cider. It may be drunk young on its own, but is more usually blended with older lambics to produce gueuze. Sometimes fruit is added, creating a second fermentation.

MALT LIQUOR

In the United States, this strong lager is often made with a high amount of sugar to produce a thin, potent brew (6–8% alcohol).

MÄRZEN

Full-bodied and copper-coloured, this 6% alcohol lager originated in Vienna, but developed in Munich as a stronger Märzen (March) brew, which was laid down in the spring to allow it to mature for drinking at the Oktoberfest.

MILD

The dominant ale in England and Wales until the 1960s, and later in some regions, it was traditionally the worker's drink and was sold on draught (draft) in pubs and clubs. It is a relatively low-gravity, malty beer, usually lightly hopped and can be dark or pale in colour. It has now vanished from many areas, surviving mainly in the industrial West Midlands and the north-west of England.

OLD ALE

This strong, matured, rich dark ale is usually sold as a seasonal beer in England, as a winter warmer. Sometimes such ales are used as stock brews for blending with fresher brews.

OUD BRUIN

Produced in the Netherlands, "Old Browns" are traditional, weak, sweetish, brown lagers.

PALE ALE

An English bottled beer, pale ale is stronger than light ale and is usually based on the brewery's best bitter.

PILSNER

Strictly, this is a golden, hoppy, aromatic lager (*below*) from Plzen. The original Pilsner Urquell is still brewed there. Czech Pilsner has a complex character with a flowery hop aroma and a dry finish. This classic drink has spawned a thousand imitators with varying results. German Pilsners are now the most dominant, and are dry and hoppy with a light golden colour, containing about 5% alcohol. They often lack the smooth maltiness of the original Czech version.

PORTER

The first mass-produced beer (*left*), porter was a traditional London brown mild ale that was much more heavily hopped than usual so that its keeping qualities were improved. It was then matured for months in vast vats to increase its alcoholic strength. Older brews were blended with fresher ones to create a combination of characteristics. Porter brews were originally highly successful, but sales gradually declined in the 19th century and only the stronger "stouter" porters survived. The name is still used around the world to indicate a brown beer.

RAUCHBIER

The intense smoky flavour of these German smoked beers from Franconia comes from malt that has been dried over moist beechwood fires. Nine breweries in the town of Bamburg produce this dark, bottom-fermented speciality.

RED BEER

The reddish colour of these sour beers of West Flanders in Belgium (*left*) comes from using Vienna malt. They are often dubbed the "Burgundies of Belgium".

ROGGEN

Only a few breweries make this German or Austrian rye beer, although some English and American breweries have now started to use rye to add flavour to the barley malt. In addition to this, there is also the odd specialist brew in production.

☆ FURTHER CLASSIFICATIONS ☆

There are numerous terms that have emerged, which signify particular general aspects of beers, rather than a particular type.

A Duppel, or Double, describes a Trappist or abbey beer from Belgium that is particularly dark and of medium strength. A Trippel, or Tripel, indicates the strongest brew in a range of beers, which tend to be hoppy, golden brews.

The term Export was originally used to denote a better-quality beer that was worth selling abroad. This term now tends to describe beers that are quite strong. Scottish brewers use the term Heavy to describe a standard strength brew, between a Light and an Export.

Urquell is the German word meaning "original source". The term should be used to show that the beer is the first in its style, such as Pilsner Urquell. Often only Ur is used, as in Einbecker Mai-Ur-Bock.

SAISON/SEZUEN

This Belgian speciality is a refreshing, slightly sour summer beer mainly made in the rural breweries of the French-speaking Wallonia region. The orange, highly hopped, top-fermenting ales are brewed in winter and laid down to condition in sturdy wine bottles for drinking in the hot summer months. They are sold in corked bottles after ageing. Some of these speciality beers contain added spices, such as ginger, and indeed, saison is a French term meaning, "season".

SCOTCH ALE

Scotland's ales tend to be more malty than English ones. The bottled Scotch ale in Belgium is a powerful rich drink, often brewed in Belgium itself.

STEAM BEER

A cross between a bottom-fermented beer and an ale, this was brewed with lager yeasts at warm temperatures in wide shallow pans in the Gold Rush days in California. Now it is brewed only by the Anchor Steam Brewery of San Francisco.

STEINBIER

"Stone beer" is heated by red-hot rocks lowered into the brew to bring it to the boil. The sizzling stones become covered in burnt sugars and are added back to the beer at maturation stage to spark a second fermentation.

STOUT

This dry black brew (*above*) is made using dark roasted barley in the mash, and is heavily hopped. It is one of the classic styles of ale, and is partly made famous through the success of Guinness. Draught (draft) stout tends to be much smoother and creamier than the more distinctive bottled beer because it uses nitrogen gas in its dispenser. Besides dry or bitter stout, there are a number of variations. Milk or sweet stout is a much weaker and smoother bottled stout, using lactose (milk sugar). Oatmeal stout, now mostly vanished, is a sweet stout containing added oats. Oyster stout is the perfect accompaniment to oysters. Some American and English brewers have occasionally revived this style, but the main, bottled, oyster stout available today does not contain any oysters. Russian or Imperial stout was originally brewed in London in the 18th century as an extra-strong export porter for the Baltic, and it is a rich, intense brew with a fruit-cake character.

TRAPPIST

This designation refers strictly to beers from the five Trappist monastery breweries in Belgium and one in the Netherlands. The range of strong and complex ales is spicy and top-fermenting. Commercial breweries producing ales in the same style or under licence have to call their brews abbey beers.

VIENNA

These amber-red lagers were produced by the Austrian brewing pioneer, Anton Dreher. They now have little to do with the city.

WEISSE OR WEIZEN

This white, wheat style of beer (*below*) is popular in Bavaria. Made with 50–60 per cent malted wheat, they are pale, often cloudy brews and are popular in the summer. They have the quenching qualities of lager, but as they are top-fermented, all the flavour of an ale. Hefeweizen is unfiltered and cloudy, Kristall is filtered. Weizenbock is a stronger brew and Dunkelweizen a dark one.

WITBIER

The white wheat beers of Belgium, also known as "Bières Blanches", are very well known. They are brewed using 50 per cent wheat, and flavoured most notably with orange peel and coriander (cilantro). They have a spicy, fruity flavour and an enticing aroma. Since Pieter Celis revived spiced wheat beer in 1966, many breweries have copied the style.

Ingredients for Beer

Beer is a much more complex drink than is often realized, and there are many mysteries hidden in a single glass, not least of which are its ingredients. Malt and hops, perhaps unfamiliar in themselves, undergo many alterations during the brewing process, from germination and roasting to mashing. Even yeast, which is the "magic" ingredient used to turn sugar to alcohol, is available in different forms that will directly influence each beer. And after all these various considerations, a beer may then be flavoured with a wide range of additional ingredients, such as cherries and other fruits or ginger.

WATER

Beer consists mainly of water – called liquor by brewers – and its quality and mineral content directly affect the character of the brew. Water contains six main component salts, and their proportions affect the flavour and sometimes the colour of the finished product. High levels of bicarbonate, for example, can produce a highly acidic mash, giving a poor rate of sugar extraction from the malt.

Many brewers now boast about the source of the water that they use, while some of the greatest brewing towns were set up around a good liquor supply. Plzen in the Czech Republic, for example, had very soft water, which was perfect for brewing Pilsner-style lagers, while the water in Burton-on-Trent in England had the right mineral content for brewing its famous pale ales. In fact, London brewers were so jealous of the water in Burton that many built their own breweries there, and a Lancashire brewer even used to transport Burton water miles to his brewery by rail.

Today, breweries all over the world that want to produce pale ales usually "Burtonize" their water first by adding gypsum salts. Burton water was drawn from deep wells in the layer of gypsum beneath the town. This fine liquid, purified by slow, natural filtration, contains high levels of calcium, which make for clear, bright bitters as it increases malt extraction during the mashing process.

Many breweries have now abandoned traditional wells and springs because of the threat of contamination. Instead, they use treated town water from the mains supply and add the minerals that they require. It is not as romantic as a well, but it is more reliable. Breweries certainly need vast amounts of water. For every litre of beer produced, at least five more are required for cleaning and cooling, so a strong water supply is a vital concern.

ABOVE: *A field of ripe barley, ready for harvesting.*

LEFT: *Water is used to germinate grains as part of the malting process.*

MALT

Malt is the body and soul of a brew, and will provide not only the alcohol but also much of the flavour and nearly all of the colour in a glass of beer. Malt is the result of a series of processes that are applied to raw grain. Raw ears of barley, for example, will barely ferment and are of little use to the brewer. First they need to pass through the hands of the maltster, who, in ten days, turns a grain of barley into a grain of malt.

When the grain arrives at the maltsters' it will first be cleaned. It is then soaked in water at regular intervals for two to three days, and spread out on huge floors to germinate, a process which turns inaccessible starches in the seeds into sugar. After five days, this "green malt" is sent to the kiln where it is baked for two days at specific temperatures. Finally, the roots from germination are removed and the malt is ready. This delicious final product is used not only to brew beer, but also to make malted drinks, biscuits and breakfast cereals, and is also used in malt whisky.

Barley is by far the most favoured cereal by brewers the world over as it provides the best extraction rate of sugars, although it is possible to malt wheat, oats or rye. German wheat beers specifically require a wheat malt, and oats were widely used for brewing during World War II when barley was scarce. Even barley itself must be specifically suitable for malting. It must have plump, sound grains that germinate at an even rate. It should also be low in nitrogen, a gas which can affect fermentation.

ABOVE RIGHT: Some key ingredients used for making beer include (from left), barley, malt and hops.

LEFT: Malt is one of the key ingredients at the heart of all good beer, such as in these Belgian Trappist ales.

The brewers' search for a particular quality of barley has resulted in an international grain market since the 19th century. Surprisingly, much of the worldwide market in barley comes from a few original varieties. In the 1820s, the Reverend J. B. Chevallier spotted a barley growing in an English labourer's cottage garden in Debenham, Suffolk. Struck with its extraordinary quality, he saved the seed and the Chevallier barley strain was developed from that. Archer was another popular English variety. The barley plant produces kernels of grain which grow in either two or six rows. Chevallier and Archer are both two-rowed barleys. In the United States, six-rowed barley is preferred.

After World War II, Archer and its hybrids Spratt-Archer and Plumage-Archer gave way to Proctor, which was better suited to mechanized farming. Modern varieties include Triumph, Kym, Klages, Halcyon and Pipkin. Some more traditional brewers have remained true to lower-yielding (for the farmer) but more characterful grains (for the brewer), such as Golden Promise.

21

☆ TYPES OF MALT ☆

Malt comes in a variety of styles, depending on how it is kilned. The higher the temperature, the darker the colour and more profound the flavour. The brewer skilfully blends different malts to produce different beers.

Pale Malt: *This is the standard malt in most beers. The barley is baked in the kiln over 48 hours with a slowly rising temperature. It is ideal for both light-coloured ales and Pilsners. Other malts are sometimes mixed with this one.*

Amber and Brown Malts: *These are in fact rarely used today. The barley is heated to higher temperatures to give more coppery colours to the brew.*

Crystal Malt: *An exceptionally rapidly rising temperature in the kiln dries out the barley husk, leaving behind a hard, sugary, crystalline core. Crystal malt adds a fuller, sweeter flavour to beer. Dark varieties are called caramel malts, while lighter ones are known as carapils malts.*

Chocolate Malt: *This generates a complex mix of roasted flavours as well as a dark colour. The barley is steadily heated to about 200°C/400°F.*

Black Malt: *This is a chocolate malt that has been taken almost to burning point. Because of its powerful bitter taste, it is used sparingly, even in stouts and porters.*

HOPS

Hops add immeasurably to the flavour of beer, imparting a bitter taste that is in demand by many drinkers, while also helping to preserve the brew. Medieval holy communities in Central Europe are credited with being the first to brew beer with hops. But while the monastic brewers may have welcomed the hop plant for its preservative values, various vested interests strongly resisted its development. The Archbishop of Cologne enjoyed a monopoly on the herbs used for flavouring beer and tried to suppress the use of hops. Only in 1500 did he agree to take a rent in lieu of his rights.

In the Netherlands in the 14th century, many drinkers developed a taste for hopped Hamburg beer from over the border in preference to their gruit (or flavoured) ales. The nobility, who had vested interests in the sale of herbs, tried to exclude foreign beers, but demand was strong and hopped beers were soon brewed.

Use of the hop soon spread from the Low Countries into England. Hopped beer was imported into Winchelsea in Sussex by 1400 and, before long, brewers from Flanders followed, setting up their own breweries, much to the disgust of the English ale makers. Their concern was understandable, for hopped beer kept much better than the sweeter ale.

The hop plant (*Humulus lupulus*) is a tall, climbing bine. Only the female flowers form the required cones. The cone is made up of petal-like structures called bracts. As they ripen, the bases of these bracts bear glands filled with a yellow resin called lupulin, which contains the alpha acids that make hops bitter.

Each year the plant is cut back to the rootstock, then in the spring shoots covered with hooked hairs, called bines, surge upwards. The hop farmer provides a support network of poles and wires for the shoots to wind around. The flowers appear in summer and are followed by the cones that are harvested in autumn.

Many traditional brewers still prefer to use whole hop cones, but processed derivatives are commonly used today. The simplest by-product is made by grinding the cones into powder, which is then pressed into pellets that are easy to use with modern equipment. However, pellets do not provide the filter bed of hops required by some older breweries. Hop extract is another alternative. It is sold in a can and is highly efficient, but has a heavy taste.

ABOVE LEFT: There are many types of malt available, including (from left) pale, crystal and chocolate malt.

ABOVE: Hordes of hop-pickers came from the cities, often using the opportunity for an annual holiday away from the grime and smoke.

LEFT: A worker rotates some dried hops in a kiln.

☆ TRADITIONAL AROMA HOPS ☆

Bramling Cross: *A 1920s cross between an English Golding and a Canadian wild hop.*
Cascade: *A fruity American aromatic hop from 1972.*
Crystal: *A mildly aromatic American hop.*
Fuggles: *Propagated by Richard Fuggle in Kent in 1875 and grown in the United Kingdom, the United States and Slovenia.*
Goldings: *Originated in East Kent and used for dry-hopping traditional English ales in the cask.*
Hallertauer Mittelfrüh: *A traditional aroma hop from Bavaria. This has been almost wiped out by disease.*
Hersbrucker: *A popular German aroma hop.*
Huller: *A new German aromatic variety developed at the Hull Research Institute in Hallerau.*
Mount Hood: *An American aroma hop from 1989.*
Perle: *A newer German aroma hop.*
Progress: *Introduced in the 1950s in England.*
Quingdao da Hau: *Derived from Styrian Goldings, this is the predominant Chinese hop.*
Saaz: *The classic aroma hop from the Czech Republic.*
Select: *An aromatic hop from the Hull Research Centre.*
Spalter: *A traditional German variety mainly grown in the Spalt region near Nuremberg.*
Styrian Goldings: *Slovenia's main aromatic hop.*
Tettnanger: *A delicately aromatic German hop.*
Tradition: *A new German hop variety.*
WGV: *Whitbread Golding's Variety was widely planted in the 1950s.*
Willamette: *An American relation to the English Fuggle, from 1976.*

YEAST

Without yeast, malt, hops and water would never make beer. It is the catalyst that transforms the hopped cereal solution into a potent drink. Yeasts are living organisms, members of the fungus family. Each plant consists of a single cell, which reproduces by budding. A bud forms on the parent, then, when it has grown to the same size, it separates to form another cell. The cells can reproduce every two hours in this way, in the right conditions, such as in a sugar solution.

During fermentation, the yeast cells will clump together. In top-fermenting beers, such as stout, they rise to the surface of the liquid, while in bottom-fermenting beers, such as lagers, they sink. The yeast receives the energy for its growth during brewing by consuming

the sugar solution in the mash provided by the malt. Alcohol and carbon dioxide are produced as waste products.

Many brewers use the same yeast for years, which is therefore jealously guarded. Each strain has its own characteristics that will produce specific types of beer. Some work quickly, while others ferment slowly.

Although pure, single yeast strains are more predictable, many brewers still prefer to use multiple yeast strains. Each reacts with the others to produce the final beer. At the end of each brew the yeast is skimmed off, ready for use in the next batch. Some brewers even leave the yeast in the beer to give extra flavour, such as the cloudy Hefe wheat beers of Germany.

Scientists have spent many years trying to uncover the workings of yeast. A Dutchman named Leeuwenhoek first described its appearance in 1685, but it was the work of Frenchman Louis Pasteur in the 19th century that explained its role in fermentation.

By examining yeast through a microscope, Pasteur demonstrated that it was a living organism and he was able to identify and isolate the contaminants that had been causing brewers so many problems. Previously, brewers often suffered great losses when their beer became sour, for no apparent reason. Pasteur's work prompted J.C. Jacobsen to build a magnificent laboratory at the Carlsberg Brewery in Copenhagen in the late 1870s, where another great scientist, Emil Hansen, was able to break yeasts down to single strains that were more dependable.

☆ LOUIS PASTEUR ☆

Louis Pasteur was already world-famous when he started to study beer in 1871. His work was motivated by national pride following France's defeat in the Franco-Prussian war. He started his researches to

benefit, "a branch of industry wherein we are undoubtedly surpassed by Germany," according to the preface to his ground-breaking work "Etudes sur la Bière", in 1876. He called his resulting brew, Bière de la Revanche Nationale *(Beer of National Revenge).*

ABOVE: *Fresh yeast turns into a frothy liquid when mixed with a warm, sugary solution.*

RIGHT: *Yeast in its dried form.*

OTHER INGREDIENTS

As well as the great variety to be found through using malt, hops and different water compositions, there are also many extra ingredients that can be added to a brew to produce a highly individual recipe. These "adjuncts" are added to the grist, when the malt is cracked in the mill. They can be used as a cheaper substitute for part of the malt or when it is in short supply. Sometimes, however, the ingredients are added to enhance the flavour of the beer.

The most common adjunct is sugar, added either in blocks or as a syrup. It ferments easily and quickly to produce more alcohol, but leaves little in the way of body. Heated sugars or caramels are sometimes used instead of coloured malts to darken beers. Belgian brewers often use a less-refined candy sugar. This adjunct is particularly favoured in Africa, where barley is scarce.

Maize (corn), usually processed into flakes, is widely used. In some American breweries it accounts for as much as half the mash, giving a dry, light-coloured beer.

Rice, like maize, can be used as a partial alternative to malt. Budweiser from the United States, one of the world's best-selling beers, uses rice to give a clean, crisp finish.

ABOVE: *Some Pyramid ales are brewed with spices.*

RIGHT: *Preparing red cherries for a Belgian beer.*

Other adjuncts include torrefied wheat, which is a heated cereal that is added to help head retention, and malt extracts, sometimes used to make a larger brew than the capacity of the mash tun allows. In addition, unmalted roasted barley is sometimes used to blacken brews. It gives a harsh, dry flavour. The classic Irish stout Guinness uses a small amount of roasted barley in the mash to give the beer its distinctive bitter flavour. Then there are flavour enhancers, such as fruit, that add a final touch.

☆ FLAVOUR ENHANCERS ☆

Adding extra flavourings to beer is an old tradition. In the days before the hop, brewers made their own flavouring, called gruit, which was often a secret mix of herbs and spices. Although the tradition has mainly died out, the Belgians never gave up their demand for age-old fruit beers.

Honey is one of the oldest flavour enhancers and it has been used in cooking and drinks for centuries. Ginger is also a well-known flavouring. Adding herbs, such as coriander (cilantro) to flavour the brew is an ancient tradition that has been revived by Hoegaarden.

Orange and lemon peel, apples, raspberries, cherries and bananas have all been added to beer with varying degrees of success. Some of the newer fruit-flavoured brews were conceived by modern marketing departments. However, some traditional recipes use the fruit to spark a natural secondary fermentation as well as to add flavour. Beers with whole chillies in the bottle (above) are a fairly new innovation. Liquorice (left) is another possible flavour enhancer.

The Craft of Brewing

In days gone by, the brewer's success depended on luck to a great extent, since the processes underlying brewing were little understood. As the industry underwent great changes during the last two centuries, brewing has become highly regulated. A recent renaissance of small localized breweries has revived some more traditional aspects of this ancient craft. However, whether brewing is carried out in an enormous city plant or in a tiny back room behind a tavern or bar, the basic processes remain the same.

EXTRACTING THE SUGARS

The first step in making beer is to extract all the sugars that are stored in the malt, whether malted barley, wheat or any other grain. The malted grain is ground in a mill. The crushed malt is known as grist. The grist is then mixed

with hot liquor (the brewer's term for water) to produce a sweet-smelling mash, which is left to settle in a vessel known as a mash tun. There are two methods of extracting the sugars from the malt, and these are infusion and decoction.

With infusion, the water, or hot liquor, is left to dissolve the sugars in the crushed malt for a couple of hours, until the

mash tun contains a warm, thick, sweet liquid called sweet wort, and the remaining soaked cereal. The sweet wort is drained away through slotted plates in the base of the mash tun. The soaked cereal that is left behind is sprayed (sparged) with more hot liquor to wring out any final lingering sugars. The spent grain by-product is then sold as cattle feed. This relatively simple system is most commonly used in ale brewing.

In the more complex decoction system, which is usually used for bottom-fermenting beers such as Pilsner beers, the mash is drawn off (decocted) from the tun, little by little at different stages. Each part is passed to a cooking vessel called a mash cooker, where it is slowly brought to the boil, in some cases through precisely controlled temperature steps. After a few minutes at boiling point, the wort is then returned to the mash tun. The aim of the decoction process is to extract as much sugar from the malt as possible by mashing at many different temperatures.

ABOVE: A 19th-century etching entitled, "The Brewer".

LEFT: A brewery worker holds a glass of beer.

RIGHT: An early illustration shows a raucous tavern scene.

Some brewers seek to maximize the rate of sugar extraction from the malt as much as possible by drawing off twice (double decoction) or sometimes even three times (triple decoction) over a period of just a few hours. Extraction is a particularly important process in lager brewing because the lighter malts, which contain less sugar, are used and so as much sugar as possible must be removed. The decoction method is most commonly used in conjunction with another filter vessel, known as the lauter tun. This tun contains a series of rotating knives or blades that keep the bottom of the mash open, and this allows the sweet wort to drain away more easily.

BREWING UP

Some of the names given to the utensils used in brewing still have a reassuring kitchen ring about them, a throwback to when brewing was a domestic chore. The brew-kettle is the vessel that the sweet wort is run into once it has been extracted from the malt, and it was once just that. It is also known as "the copper", because traditionally it was made of shining copper.

Today, in the large breweries the brew kettles are usually closed and heated by internal steam coils. This is where the actual process of "brewing" takes place, as the liquid is boiled with the hops for an hour or more. Some hops are added at the start of the boil to help clarify the wort and impart bitterness. Late copper hops are sometimes added nearer the end and boiled just long enough to release their oils to provide the final aroma.

TURNING SUGAR TO ALCOHOL

After the boiling is complete, the hopped wort passes through a filtering device, known as a hopback, to remove the spent hops. It may also be passed through a whirlpool or centrifuge to remove unwanted proteins before it is cooled for the fermentation. Originally, the brew would have been cooled in large, open trays, but in modern breweries, heat exchangers (paraflows) or chilling devices are usually used in order to speed up the process.

ABOVE: Coppers at a brewery in China.

LEFT: The Guinness brewery, Dublin, in 1953.

RIGHT: An advertisement for an English brewery.

☆ THE BURTON UNION SYSTEM ☆

In the Burton Union brewing system, the beer is fermented in several linked oak casks – in union – with the fermenting beer rising through a swan-neck pipe connecting each cask to a top trough which runs the length of the whole system. The beer then runs back down from the trough, leaving any excess yeast behind. This constant circulation while the beer is fermenting ensures a vigorous result and is effective because it fully aerates the beer, giving the yeast the right amount of oxygen to work properly.

The Burton-on-Trent giants Bass dropped the Burton Union System in 1982, claiming that it had become too expensive to maintain. In contrast, the traditional Marston's brewery has invested heavily in new unions, which it still uses in order to brew its Owd Rodger and some of its Pedigree.

Once in the fermentation vessels, the yeast is pitched in. The millions of tiny cells begin to feast on the sugarwort for four to eight days, turning the sugars to alcohol and producing carbon-dioxide gas. In top-fermenting ales, the yeast rises to create a heaving head that may need skimming to prevent it from over-flowing. In bottom-fermenting beers, the yeast sinks.

Fermentation vessels range in size and shape from small, wooden rounds to vast stainless steel tanks. In the simplest and oldest systems, large barrels are used for fermentation and the yeast bubbles up through the bung hole in the top. Modern breweries tend to prefer huge enclosed conical fermenters, stacked like upright rockets alongside the brewhouse. When fermentation is complete, the yeast is drained from the bottom of the vessels.

MATURING AND CONDITIONING

After the initial, vigorous fermentation, the liquid, which is known as "green beer", is run into conditioning tanks where it is left to settle and mature. The length, nature and location of this final process differ from beer to beer. For some ales, such as mild ones, this period is short. For bottom-fermenting beers, the process takes place at temperatures close to freezing and can last for many weeks, even months, cleaning the brew and slowly completing the fermentation. Conditioning builds up the beer's carbon dioxide, the gas that will give the beer its head in the glass when poured.

RIGHT: Yeast being skimmed from the top of a fermenting vessel at the Young's brewery, in London.

MIDDLE RIGHT: A mash tun, where malt is mixed with the water, known as hot liquor.

FAR RIGHT: A copper, where hops are added to and boiled with the wort.

Some brewers add a portion of young, vigorously fermenting wort to the green beer to stimulate a final fermentation. This is known as krausening. The modern, industrial alternative is to pump in extra carbon dioxide.

Most beers are filtered between conditioning and packaging at the brewery. Some breweries use a natural mineral, known as kieselguhr, on fine mesh screens; others use fine sheet filters. Some traditional beers are racked directly into wooden or metal casks or bottles ready to go to the customer without filtration or any other processing. These beers are known as cask- or bottle-conditioned brews. Finings (a glutinous substance that is made from fish swim-bladders) are also added to the cask to clear the beer.

The brew may also be primed with sugar in the bottle or cask in order to encourage further fermentation. Dry hops may be added to the cask to give the beer more aroma. Some brewers even add extra yeast at this stage. Cask-conditioned or bottle-conditioned brews continue to mature until they are served.

HI-TECH BREWING

The driving force in the brewing industry has been to improve efficiency and reduce overheads. There has certainly been a great deal of success in increasing the amount of control the brewers have.

The chemistry and biological actions involved in making a brew are now clearly understood and major brewers leave as little as possible to chance, using science to monitor and regulate the progress and content of each brew. Huge plants are run by banks of computers and the increase in the scale of brewing has reduced the cost to the producer of each final

ABOVE: Nowadays, large breweries control the brewing process through a complex system of computerization. This regulates and controls the vast output that needs to be managed.

☆ A UNIQUE TECHNIQUE ☆

When Fritz Maytag bought the bankrupt Anchor brewery in San Francisco in 1965, his main aim was to preserve a piece of Californian history. This brewery used a unique American method of brewing perfected in the California Gold Rush days when no refrigeration was available. Shallow fermenters cooled the brew, producing a cross between a lager and an ale.

Maytag maintained this tradition and his Anchor Steam Beer gained a national reputation. It helped inspire the new brewery movement by showing that quality beers of character had a market in America.

pint. However, few of the technological advances that have been made have provided a major step forward in quality.

Normally, brewing is done by the batch method. Individual brews are put through the process, from raw ingredients to the finished product, one after another. This system means that for some period, the equipment for each stage is unused while it waits for the next batch to arrive. It is also necessary to clean and prepare the vessels so that they are ready for the next batch.

Of course, in a large-scale operation, this period of waiting is minimized because the batches are sent through quickly, one after the other. However, some companies felt they could make enor-

mous savings in cost if they could introduce continuous brewing, with wort and fermenting beer continually flowing through the plant. This method was pioneered by Morton Coutts of Dominion Breweries of New Zealand in the 1950s. Watney's developed a similar system in England in the 1970s. However, this did not provide the expected savings and the resulting flavour of the beer was somewhat disappointing.

High-gravity brewing is yet another method of increasing output that has been more widely adopted. In this system, the beer is first produced at a higher strength than is intended for the finished product. The brew is then diluted with water at the end to bring it down to the required gravity.

High-gravity brewing allows the brewer to produce more beer than was previously possible in the same plant. Some companies are now investigating extending this concept by brewing just one high-gravity bland brew, which can then be diluted to produce different strength beers and then through the addition of different flavourings, colourings and extracts, be used to produce a range of different products.

☆ THE BURGUNDIES OF FLANDERS ☆

At the Rodenbach brewery in Belgium, a reasonably conventional ale is brewed, using Vienna crystal malt to impart a red colour. However, Rodenbach's distinct character arises from the way it is then matured. After a second fermentation, the beer is left in huge oak tuns for at least 18 months. During this time, it ages and sours. The inside of the tun is uncoated, so the beer is also flavoured through direct contact with the wood. Rodenbach produces only three beers – Rodenbach, Grand Cru and Alexander – sometimes called the Burgundies of Flanders. Other more conventional breweries have attempted to imitate these classic ales, but rarely use the same demanding craft.

BIO-SCIENCE AT WORK

Advances in bio-technology and genetics mean that it is now possible to manipulate and control the process of fermentation by changing the nature of the yeast. Enzymes have been used by some brewers, notably in

ABOVE: *Casks being filled with traditional draught (draft) beer at Young's brewery.*

RIGHT: *A bottle of Grolsch, a beer that does not have its flavour altered by the process of pasteurization.*

the United States, to speed up the brewing process. Biological science has also been used in the fight against contamination, in the form of techniques for disinfecting and cleaning equipment.

It is now common practice for manufacturers to attempt to prolong the shelf-life and stability of their beer products through pasteurization. Virtually all canned and many bottled beers are pasteurized, as are pressurized keg beers for serving at the bar.

During pasteurization the beer is heated to kill off any dangerous bacteria that may have entered it during the brewing process

and that may turn it sour. One method of pasteurizing is to spray the bottles or cans with hot water for about an hour. Another method is to spray extremely hot water or steam over a can or bottle for about a minute.

Pasteurization does, however, have its problems. Not only does the process eradicate any unwanted organisms, but it also kills the yeast and, inevitably, the flavour and character of the beer are affected. As a result, most pasteurized beers are usually artificially carbonated in order to give them a semblance of life when they are served and to ensure a satisfactory head on the glass.

Louis Pasteur, was also aware of such difficulties. In a footnote to the english edition of *"Etudes sur la Bière"* he explains, "This process is less successful in the case of beer than in that of wine, for the delicacy of flavour which distinguishes beer is affected by the heat". For many beer drinkers this process has remained problematic and some leading lager brewers, such as Grolsch, have bowed to demands and demonstrated that it is possible even for widely distributed beers to remain unpasteurized.

ABOVE: A traditional bar in Ireland.

LEFT: A few english breweries still deliver local beer by horse-drawn dray.

RIGHT: Checking the casks in a brewery.

From Cask to Glass

Until well into the 20th century, beer was often served at the bar or directly from the wooden casks that rested on the stillage, a wooden frame-work. If the casks were in the cellar, a pump would be used to raise the beer to the bar.

Making the wooden casks was called cooper-ing. This was a highly skilled craft as casks had to be strong and leak-proof. In the 1930s, metal-made casks were introduced. These lighter and cheaper versions slowly replaced wooden casks, apart from within some more traditional breweries.

BOTTLED BEER

The brewing industry has long sought to provide containers for customers to carry their beer. Earthenware vessels date back cen-turies and glass bottles have been used since the 17th century.

Bottled beer became more common in the 19th century, with mechanization, and brew-ers began to develop their dis-tinctive shapes. Bottles were usually brown or green to pre-vent light penetrating them. They were corked like wine bottles, until screw stoppers were introduced in 1872. The metal crown cap then came 20 years later and its cheapness suited mass-production.

THE SIX-PACK

The tin can appeared in the 1930s, although foods had been sold in cans since the early 19th century. Glass bottles were cheaper and did not taint the taste of the beer, so breweries were not interested. Beer sales in the United States shot up after Prohibition, and a manufacturer called CanCo developed a tin can with an internal lining that was capable of resisting the pressure of beer. In January 1935, the first canned brands were launched.

Cans were lighter to carry and fitted easily into the refrigera-tors that were now appearing in every kitchen. Today, cans (made from aluminium) are widely used and trends for availability include the six- and four-packs, although many breweries still pre-sent their beers in bottles due to popular demand.

The "widget" was invented in the early 1990s in an attempt to retain the feel of a draught (draft) beer in the can in Britain. This small, plastic device injects nitrogen into the beer when opened, to provide it with a creamy, thick head. However, it is doubtful that this has improved the taste of beer.

ABOVE: Transporting casks in 1805.

LEFT: Monitoring the bottling process of Tennent's lager.

RIGHT: Beer is readily available in cans, although many breweries prefer to use traditional bottling methods.

A BEER BY ANY OTHER NAME

However good the beer, people cannot buy it if they have not heard of it or do not remember its name. Much thought goes into naming beers and today, even more into advertising and marketing them. The Japanese Spring Valley brewery adopted the name Kirin for its beers in 1888. This fabled animal – half dragon, half horse – is regarded as a symbol of good luck and is used to establish a brand identity. Similarly, Budweiser, one of the world's leading beer brands, is named after the famous town in the Czech Republic, a name redolent with brewing history. A number of breweries have opted for a note of comedy in their title – The Bishop's Tipple, Indiana's Bones, Loaded Dog and La Fin du Monde.

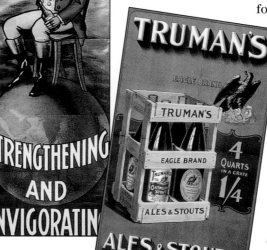

Making your beer stand out from all others is crucial to breweries and producing the right label for a brand is vital. Beer mats – witty, attractive, informative, puzzling and in collectors' series – are an inexpensive and popular way of doing this. "Breweriana", or the habit of collecting the marketing paraphernalia used by brewers to promote their beers, is an international hobby. Collectibles include beer mats, postcards, watches and foam skimmers.

Decorated, branded and shaped glasses, while being expensive to produce, also effectively distinguish beers at a glance. Most Belgian beers are accompanied by their own glass. Everyone in the bar will know what is being drunk.

Dublin's Guinness brewery was one of the first to achieve international fame. In spite of its huge success, it never ceased its distinctive advertising campaigns, which have become known the world over. It has used many slogans, but "Guinness is good for you" and other variations, have made a lasting impact.

ABOVE LEFT: A bottle of the popular Japanese beer, Kirin.

LEFT: Memorable examples of "breweriana" include (from top) an old Budweiser label, and two beer mats – the Czech beer Gambrinus and the Canadian Eau Bénite.

CENTRE: Early English and Irish beer advertisements.

ABOVE: The wittily named Bishop's Tipple.

BELOW: A few of the distinctively shaped glasses that are designed for serving particular beers.

Serving and Drinking Beer

Asking for a beer is a vague statement of intent. Many drinkers take beer for granted, assuming that a glass has little to offer beyond quenching a thirst and providing intoxication. But beer is much more than a chilled Pilsner on a hot day.

You should never rush a good beer. The anticipation is part of the enjoyment. Take the trouble to pour the beer carefully into a clean glass, ensuring a reasonable head. First drink with your eyes and appreciate the colours in your beer – even a dark stout conceals a ruby in its depths. Don't necessarily worry if the beer is not sparkling and bright. Some brews, such as yeasty wheat beers from Germany, are meant to be cloudy. Then, savour the aroma. Some beers have a subtle scent, while others can be overpowering, but each should be enticing. At last, let the beer flow right over your tongue to pick up all the different taste sensations. Now swallow, then wait a little, so that each of the flavours that are left behind are

savoured. A good beer should linger long on the palate, and the taste should not be strangled in your throat.

Generally speaking, the best beer of most styles is on draught (draft). It is at the heart of the community in many countries, such as in a cosy English pub, a huge German beer cellar, a packed Czech bar or a roadside bar in Africa. Tasting local beer is often a good way to meet the locals, who will probably know where to find the best brews available.

There is a suitable beer for almost every occasion: ice-cold lager is perfect for the beach; a pink framboise makes an excellent aperitif; a bock is best enjoyed in a beer hall at a festival; and a stout is ideal by the fire on a cool evening, in a country pub.

ABOVE: Watching a Pilsner being poured is so enticing.

LEFT: Drinking in a crowded beer tent at the Oktoberfest in Munich, Germany.

RIGHT: Serving a pint of beer from the tap needs a certain amount of skill in order to achieve the right head.

BEER GLASSES

There is now a great variety of beer glass styles to choose from. Most beers can actually be savoured quite happily from any clean glass and there are not really any strict and essential rules.

However, there are some glass shapes that have developed in order to complement certain types of beer, particularly in Belgium. It is therefore worth going to the effort of selecting the most suitable, if possible, to enjoy your beer to its full capacity.

ABOVE: *This tall, long glass is ideal for lighter beers such as Pilsners and witbiers.*

ABOVE: *A wide-bowled goblet, for aromatic beers and strong ales, similar to the Duvel tulip.*

ABOVE: *A beer flute is an elegant glass, ideally suited to Belgian fruit beers.*

ABOVE: *Tall, thick glasses are ideal for keeping Oktoberfest and witbiers nice and cool.*

ABOVE: *An english pub glass can be used for most beers, from light beers to ales or bitters.*

ABOVE: *A simple tumbler that is similar in its usage to the english pub glass.*

ABOVE: *This glass has become associated with stouts in particular, such as Guinness.*

A World A to Z of Beers

This journey around the world of beer gives a glimpse into the thousands of brews that can be found today. Presented in alphabetical order, the special selection includes a range of notable brands from around the globe, complete with informative notes on tasting.

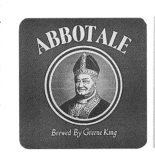 

AASS BOCK (NORWAY)

A creamy, copper-coloured, malty bock beer (6.1%) from the Aass brewery in Drammen, which is Norway's oldest brewery. It offers ten different brews, including Classic Special Brygg, an aromatic, dark-gold lager (4.5%) with a crisp, clean hop taste.

ABBOT ALE (ENGLAND)

This robust and bright-amber, fruity premium bitter (5%) from Greene King is named after the last abbot of Bury St Edmunds in East Anglia, the brewer's home town. In 1995, this East Anglian giant added a new range of seasonal cask ales to its well-known IPA and Abbot Ale.

ACME PALE ALE (UNITED STATES)

This rather famous Californian brand was revived in 1996 by North Coast, the award-winning Californian brewery in Fort Bragg, which began as a brew pub in 1988.

ADNAMS BITTER (ENGLAND)

Adnams bitter is a dark-gold classic of its type (3.7%), with a hoppy, orangey flavour. Adnams of Southwold, Suffolk, also brews a smooth, malty, dark mild (3.2%). Its Extra (4.3%), a best bitter, was voted Champion Beer of Britain in 1993.

AGNUS DEI (BELGIUM)

This complex, strong, pale tripel (8%) is an abbey-style beer from the Du Bocq brewery, sold under the Corsendonk name in Namur. This family brewery produces an excellent range of ales, under a variety of names. It is best known for its La Gauloise beers, a wheat beer, Blanche de Namur and a spicy, hoppy Saison Régal.

ALIMONY ALE (UNITED STATES)

"The bitterest beer in America" was originally brewed by beer enthusiast Bill Owens of California to mark a divorce.

AMSTEL BEER (HOLLAND)

Heineken's second-string brand name covers a range of beers, including a light lager, a hoppy Amstel 1870 (5%), the stronger Amstel Gold (7%), a robust dark and malty Amstel bokbier (7%) and the pale Amstel Lentebok (7%).

ANCHOR LIBERTY ALE
(UNITED STATES)

A strong, hazy bronze American IPA (6.1%) with a big malty hop nose, a powerful malt flavour with spicy hops, and a grapefruit finish. This is the first American beer to be dry-hopped in modern times. It is one of the best IPAs available.

ANCHOR STEAM BEER
(UNITED STATES)

A bright, copper-coloured cross between an ale and a lager (5%) with a well-rounded, malty taste and a crisp finish. Fritz Maytag's brewery of San Francisco revived this gold-rush-era beer, produced

with a shallow-fermenter brewing method by forty-niners when no refrigeration was available. The brewery has added a range of other brews, including Anchor Porter (6.3%) and Old Foghorn (8.7%).

ASAHI BLACK BEER (JAPAN)

Many Japanese like to blend this sweetish, red-brown beer (5%) with a light lager. Asahi Stout, another traditional brew, is a richly roasted, top-fermented potent stout (8%). The huge success of Super Dry since its launch in 1987, has made Asahi Japan's second largest brewing group.

AUGSBURGER (UNITED STATES)

This is the brand name for the speciality German-style beers from the United States' fourth largest brewer, Stroh, including an Alt and a Döppelbock. Augsburger beers were originally developed by the Wisconsin brewer, Huber.

BALLANTINE'S ALE
(UNITED STATES)

Once one of the best-selling ales in the United States, Ballantine's was originally brewed in Albany, New York, in the 1830s before moving to Newark, New Jersey. In the 20th century, the beers have been brewed by a variety of companies but are now produced by Pabst in Milwaukee. The best-known Ballantine beer is the copper-coloured hoppy IPA, but there is also a lighter Ballantine Ale.

BEAMISH STOUT (IRELAND)

The chocolatey Beamish Stout (4.2%) is the only stout that is just brewed within Ireland. In fact, it is not even brewed outside the town of Cork. Its distinctive flavour is partly due to the use of malted wheat as well as barley in the mash. It is exported to Britain, Europe and North America. The brewery also makes Beamish Red Ale, a smooth traditional Irish-style ale (4.5%) that has a rich red colour and a full sweet flavour.

BECK'S (GERMANY)

This is one of Germany's best-known beers on the international market. It is a crisp, dry Pilsner (5%) and has been brewed in the northern port of Bremen since 1874. It is Germany's leading export beer, with over six million hec-tolitres (a hectolitre is 26.4 gallons) sold every year in more than 100 countries. It accounts for more than 85 per cent of German beer exports to the United States. Beck's also brews a deep-amber, dark beer as well as a dry and malty special Oktoberfest brew.

BELLE-VUE (BELGIUM)

Gueuze, kriek and frambozen (5.2%) from this large-scale brewer of lambic beers are pleasant but a little undemanding. It also brews an excellent, unfiltered Séléction Lambic (5.2%) at its traditional plant in Molenbeek. Belle-Vue exports its beers to France under the Bécasse brand name.

BINTANG (INDONESIA)

A light, malty lager (5%) with a Dutch influence in its taste, from Bintang, Indonesia.

BISHOP'S TIPPLE, THE (ENGLAND)

A strong, rich, deep-amber barley wine (6.5%) with a sweet and smoky, complex flavour, once brewed within sight of the Salisbury cathedral by Gibbs Mew.

BLANCHE DE CHAMBLY (CANADA)

A cloudy, spicy, bottle-conditioned wheat beer (5%) from the Unibroue micro-brewery in Montreal. This tart, refreshing brew won the Silver Medal in the 1995 World Beer Championship. Founded by Belgian beer enthusiast André Dijon, Unibroue produces a range of quite characterful beers that are exported to France, such as Eau Bénite.

BODDINGTONS (ENGLAND)

A straw-coloured brew (3.8%) from this famous Manchester brewery. It was once worshipped for its parch-dry bitterness, but it now has a smoother flavour.

BRAINS SA (WALES)

The best-known beer from Brains of Cardiff is a dark-amber, malty, fruity premium bitter (4.2%). This traditional family brewery also produces a lightly hopped, dark mild (3.5%) called Brains Dark and a best-selling bitter (3.7%).

BRUGS TARWEBIER (BELGIUM)

Also known as Blanche de Bruges, this cloudy wheat beer (5%) is the best-known brew from Gouden Boom in Bruges. Tarwe is Belgian for "wheat".

BUSH (BELGIUM)

The strongest beer in Belgium, Bush (12%) is an amber-coloured, English-style barley wine from the Dubuisson brewery in Pipaix, Hainaut. Originally brewed in 1933, this dry, warming brew with a mellow, oaky taste became the family firm's regular beer. It is sold as Scaldis in the United States to avoid confusion with the brewing giant Anheuser-Busch. Dubuisson also brews a dark-amber Bush Noël at Christmas. In 1994, the brewery launched a weaker, hoppy Bush Beer (7%) to celebrate its 225th anniversary.

☆ PHILANTHROPIC LAGER ☆

The Carlsberg brewery was founded by Jacob Christian Jacobson on a hill at Valby just outside Copenhagen, in Denmark. It was named in honour of the founder's son, Carl, and the Danish word meaning "hill".

Jacobson was very determined to brew the bottom-fermented lagers rather than the top-fermented wheat beers widely produced by many small Danish breweries, so he travelled to Munich to study under Gabriel Sedlmayr of the Spaten brewery. Apparently, he returned from a trip in 1845 with 2 litres (3½ pints) of the essential bottom-fermenting yeast, which he kept cool throughout the long stagecoach journey by frequent dousings with cold water and then covering the containers with his stovepipe hat.

After successful experiments to produce the dark, Bavarian lager, using the cellars under the city ramparts, Jacobson brewed the first batch at his plant at Valby in 1847.

Jacobson became a leading figure of the new science of brewing and built some laboratories that became famous. It was there that in 1883, Emil Hansen isolated the first single-cell yeast culture – called Saccharomyces carlsbergensis. In 1876, Jacobson also established the Carlsberg Foundation to promote scientific research and, after his death in 1887, the foundation became the owner of the brewery.

Often in opposition to his father, Carl set up his own brewery on an adjoining site specifically for brewing Pilsners. Always more artistically inclined, he designed a new brewhouse in 1901. The Carlsberg Foundation took over this cathedral of beer in 1902, with its Florentine flourishes and four stone elephants guarding the gates. Today, the company is uniquely run as a charity for the benefit of the sciences and, since Carl's intervention, the arts as well.

CAFFREY'S IRISH ALE (IRELAND)

This strong and creamy Irish ale (4.8%) is brewed at Bass's Ulster brewery in County Antrim and now in England. It is named after Thomas R. Caffrey, who founded the brewery in 1891. Caffrey's pours like an old-fashioned stout and takes about three minutes to settle from a creamy liquid to a rich auburn colour, topped with a creamy head. The beer is served chilled.

CALEDONIAN (SCOTLAND)

Beers from the Caledonian brewery, Edinburgh, include the dark, malty 60/- beer (3.2%) with a hint of roast barley, the more creamy Caledonian 70/- (3.5%), which has a tawnier colour, and the more complex Caledonian 80/- (4.1%).

CAMEL BEER (SUDAN)

This is the Blue Nile brewery's famous Sudanese lager brand. It was first launched in 1955. The recipe was originally based on an early English lager, brewed by the Barclay Perkins company, which was widely exported to Africa from London at the time.

CASTLE LAGER (SOUTH AFRICA)

This pale, lemony-tasting lager (5%) with a dry, hoppy finish is the leading beer brand from South African Breweries. It is brewed using barley malt, maize and sucrose. The name comes from the Castle brewery founded by Charles Glass in Johannesburg in 1884. Castle Lager was the first bottom-fermenting beer produced in Africa, using a plant bought by the South African Breweries pioneer, Frederick Mead, from the United States. Once introduced in 1898, the lager proved to be such a popular refreshing drink in the hot

☆ SCOTTISH SHILLINGS ☆

Generally speaking, Scotland does not use the terms mild or bitter that are common south of its border. Instead, cask beers are traditionally rated in strength according to the invoice price charged per barrel in the 19th century.

Under the "shilling system", the weakest beer is 60/-, an average strength beer 70/- and a premium brew 80/-. Strong ales are labelled at 90/-.

African climate that South African Breweries decided to adopt the Castle name for all of its beers and breweries. Rival breweries, impressed by the success of the golden brew, rushed to imitate the trend and brew lager as well.

CASTLEMAINE XXXX (AUSTRALIA)

Still described in Australia as a bitter ale, Castlemaine XXXX is a malty golden lager (4.8%), which uses whole hops rather than pellets or hop extracts. In addition to this, the Brisbane brewery brews an all-malt Castlemaine Malt 75 (4.8%), a Castlemaine Special Dry (5%), a low-carbohydrate Castlemaine DL (4.1%), XXXX Gold (3.5%), a low-alcohol Light (2.7%) and XL (2.3%).

CELIS WHITE (UNITED STATES)

This is a Belgian-style wheat beer (5%), flavoured with coriander (cilantro) and orange peel, from the Celis brewery in Austin, Texas. Peter Celis, having revived the "white" wheat-beer style in his native Belgium, sold his brewery in Hoegaarden and decided to cross the Atlantic. He opened the Celis Brewery in 1992, brewing the wheat beer he had previously exported to the United States. Now owned by Miller, the Celis brewery brews other Belgian-style beers: Celis Raspberry (5%), a richer Grand Cru (8.7%), a Pilsner Celis Golden (5%) and a Pale Bock (5%).

CH'TI (FRANCE)

This beer's name is local Picardy patois meaning a "French north-easterner" and is the brand name for the bières de garde produced by the Castelain brewery of Bénifontaine. The rich fruity beers from this region include a deep-gold, very malty, fruity blonde and a darker brune version (both 6.5%), as well as a deep-amber-coloured Ch'ti Amber (5.9%).

CHIMAY PREMIÈRE (BELGIUM)

This is a rich, red-brown Trappist ale (7%) with a spicy, fruity flavour, from the Abbaye de Notre-Dame de Scourmont. It is known as Chimay Rouge in the 33cl bottle. A Chimay Blanche, or Cinq Cents, is a golden amber tripel (8%). Chimay Bleu, or Grand Réserve is a rich, fruity, complex ale (9%).

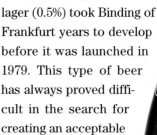

☆ **BEER BOP** ☆

The independent Josef Sigl brewery in Austria, established in 1601, makes arguably the best Pilsner in Austria, Trumer Pils. As well as a pioneering range of wheat beers, the company is also famous for its unusual labels that feature trendy characters in a special "beer bop" collection.

CHRISTOFFEL BLOND (HOLLAND)

This quality all-malt, bottom-fermented beer (5%) is dry and heavily hopped. Unfiltered and unpasteurized, it is available in bottle-conditioned form, including 2-litre (3.5-pint) swing-stoppered jugs. The small brewery, established in 1986 by Leo Brand, also produces a good Munich-style lager. Its Pilsners are regarded as some of the best in the world.

CLAUSTHALER (GERMANY)

This pioneering non-alcohol lager (0.5%) took Binding of Frankfurt years to develop before it was launched in 1979. This type of beer has always proved difficult in the search for creating an acceptable taste, and so the success of this beer has meant that it has virtually created a whole new beer sector and market on its own.

COBRA (INDIA)

This is one of the best-known lagers from India (5%) and is brewed in Bangalore, specifically for export to the West.

BREWED ☆ IN HOLLAND ☆

When Gerard Adriaan Heineken bought the Haystack brewery, the largest in Amsterdam, in December 1863, he wanted to tackle the problem of alcoholism by offering the public a light beer as an alternative to the widely popular strong spirits, like gin. He found a ready market and soon moved to a larger brewery.

In 1886, Heineken employed Dr Elion, a pupil of Louis Pasteur, to develop a consistent Pilsner, which is the hallmark of Heineken's brews.

Heineken was successfully exporting from the early years. Today, it is the leading imported brand in the United States. The company has acquired stakes in local breweries all over the world and built foreign plants, and it now has over 100 breweries around the world. Since the early 1990s, it has also started to produce all-malt beers in a wider variety of styles.

COORS (UNITED STATES)

Coors boasts the biggest single brewery in the world, dominating the town of Golden, near Denver, Colorado. Using Rocky mountain spring water, it brews a very light Coors lager and a slightly fuller-flavoured Coors Gold.

CORSENDONK (BELGIUM)

These two abbey beers in their stylish brown bottles date from as recently as 1982. They are named after the former Corsendonk Augustinian priory near Turnhout, which was established in the 15th century and was recently restored. The brews are the brainchild of a member of the well-known brewing family, Jozef Keersmaekers. The dark, chocolatey dubbel, Pater Noster, is brewed by the Van Steenberge brewery. The stronger, pale tripel, Agnus Dei (8%), is brewed at the Du Bocq brewery.

COOPERS SPARKLING ALE (AUSTRALIA)

Coopers' best-known, yeasty, cloudy brew (5.8%) is a full-flavoured, bottle-conditioned strong pale ale. Coopers also brews a richly roasted, robust Coopers Best Extra Stout (6.8%) and a fruity middle-strength Coopers Original Pale Ale (4.5%). There is also a filtered ale, Coopers Premium Clear (4.9%). All the beers are free of additives and preservatives.

COURAGE BEST (ENGLAND)

A traditional golden-brown, malty, dry cask bitter (4%). Brewed by Courage in Tadcaster, which was founded in London in 1787, it also produces a full-bodied bitter, Courage Directors (4.8%).

42

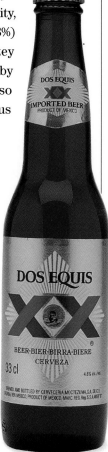

DE KONINCK (BELGIUM)

This all-malt, top-fermenting ale (5%) has been described as a cross between an English bitter and a German alt. It is matured in the cask, then pasteurized in the bottle. The stronger version is called Cuvée de Koninck (8%).

DIEBELS ALT (GERMANY)

A brown, biscuity altbier (4.8%) from the Privatbrauerei Diebel in Issum Weidernhein. It also produces light and low-alcohol versions of its altbier.

DIEKIRCH (LUXEMBOURG)

One of Luxembourg's biggest three breweries, this company has brewed in Diekirch since 1871. Besides Diekirch Light (2.9%) and the pale Diekirch Premium Pilsner (4.8%), it brews a mellow lager, Diekirch Exclusive (5.1%), the amber Diekirch Grande Réserve (6.9%) and a brune (5.2%).

DIRECTOR'S (ENGLAND)

A traditional, rich, cask bitter (4.8%) brewed in Tadcaster by Courage.

DOGBOLTER (AUSTRALIA)

A powerful ale (7%), Dogbolter was initially brewed at the Sail and Anchor brewpub in Fremantle in 1983, but is now a bottom-fermenting, creamy, dark lager from CUB-owned Matilda Bay Brewing Co. of Perth. The beer is cask-matured before bottling and takes twice as long to ferment as most Australian beers.

DOS EQUIS (MEXICO)

Dos Equis ("Two Crosses") is a rich, dark-red, high-quality, Vienna-style lager (4.8%) with a fruity, chocolatey taste. Brewed in Mexico by Moctezuma, it has also proved popular in various export markets.

DOUBLE DIAMOND (ENGLAND)

Ind Coope's famous dark-amber and bottled pale ale from Burton-on-Trent, which after a period of promotion as a weak keg beer, has seen its reputation restored as a bottled ale (4%), particularly in the stronger export version (5.2%). It is also occasionally available as a cask beer.

DOUBLE DRAGON (WALES)

Felinfoel's famous full-bodied premium bitter (4.2%) won the Challenge cup for cask beer at the Brewers' Exhibition in London in 1976. A stronger version of the dark-amber, moderately malty, delicately hopped brew from Llanelli is bottled for export, mainly to the United States.

DRAGON STOUT (JAMAICA)

A deep-brown, sweetish, rich, malty stout (7.5%). It is brewed in Kingston, Jamaica, by Desnoes & Geddes. This potent brew is believed by some to aid virility.

DRAUGHT BASS (ENGLAND)

This superb bitter (4.4%) has a malty flavour and a light hop bitterness. It used to be the biggest-selling premium ale in the country.

DUVEL (BELGIUM)

This is a beer with a devil of a reputation, one of the best-known and most celebrated drinks in Belgium. A golden ale with a frothy white top, it appears attractive but unremarkable in its balloon goblets, apart from its surging lines of bubbles. However, just one sniff of its heady hop aroma and one taste of its complex fruity flavour, together with its sustaining strength (8.5%), make the beer drinker appreciate that this is a glass apart. Duvel is brewed by the Moortgat brewery in Breendonk. After World War I, the brewery attempted to brew a Scotch ale. The Moortgat brewers examined bottles of

McEwan's ale from Edinburgh and made a dark ale using the McEwan's yeast. "It's a devil of a brew," claimed one taster, and the name Duvel was born in 1923. In 1968 Moortgat perfected a golden version. Today, the devil appears in two guises: the delicious bottle-conditioned brew has a red-lettered label; a blander, filtered version has green letters.

EB SPECJAL PILS (POLAND)

The mild, fresh, yellow-coloured lager (5.4%) is the flagship brew from Elblag's brewery. It is a triple-filtered beer, and the liquor (water) with which it is made is drawn from the brewery's very own deep wells.

EDELWEISS (AUSTRIA)

Austria's most popular range of wheat beers is produced for the Brau AG group by Hofbräu Kaltenhausen of Hallein near Salzburg. The beers tend to be lighter in flavour than their Bavarian counterparts and there is a full range: cloudy-gold Edelweiss Hefetrüb with a spicy, malt taste, filtered (and therefore clear); bright Edelweiss Kristallklar; and dark-amber Edelweiss Dunkel (all 5.5%). There is also a stronger Edelweiss Bock (7.1%).

EDINBURGH STRONG ALE (SCOTLAND)

A strong, premium ale (6.4%) with a complexity of malt and hop flavours, but without the usual sweetness of stronger beers. It is brewed by Caledonian.

EINBECKER UR-BOCK (GERMANY)

This bright-gold and smooth, strong, hoppy bock beer (6.5%) is produced within the Einbecker brewery. It also produces a deep, golden-amber, malty, spring bock (6.5%) as well as Einbecker Maibock (6.5%), a seasonal brew.

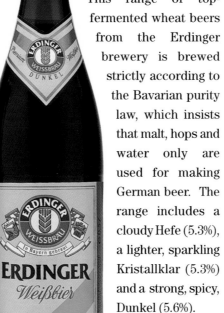

ERDINGER WEISSBIER (GERMANY)

This range of top-fermented wheat beers from the Erdinger brewery is brewed strictly according to the Bavarian purity law, which insists that malt, hops and water only are used for making German beer. The range includes a cloudy Hefe (5.3%), a lighter, sparkling Kristallklar (5.3%) and a strong, spicy, Dunkel (5.6%).

ESB (ENGLAND)

This is a much revered and strong beer. Extra Special Bitter (5.5%) from Fuller's of London has great character with a complex malt, fruit and hops flavour, and it has won the Champion Beer of Britain title an unprecedented three times. In fact, the three main brews of this London family brewer – Chiswick Bitter, London Pride and ESB – have won many more awards at the Great British Beer Festival than the beers of any other brewer.

COMMEMORATIVE ☆ BEERS ☆

Brewers often make one-off brews to commemorate special events. Harveys of Lewes in Sussex, England, bottled a special strong pale ale, the Firecracker, in honour of the emergency services who fought to save the brewery from a fire disaster in 1996. Many British brewers bottled ales to keep for the Queen's Coronation in 1953 and subsequent royal marriages. Some companies celebrate anniversaries and other celebrations with new brews, as did Channel 4.

ESTRELLA DAMM (SPAIN)

This bright-gold, honeyish, premium-quality Pilsner (5.4%) is one of Damm's best-known beers. "Star" lager is very thirst-quenching, and is intended to be served cold on a hot day. A "light", low calorie version is also available (3.2%).

FLOREFFE (BELGIUM)

This range of quality bottle-conditioned abbey beers from the Lefebvre family brewery at Quenast, south-west of Brussels, is named after the Norbertine

☆ SORGHUM BEERS ☆

Brewing using sorghum and relying on spontaneous fermentation has long been a domestic industry in Africa and it is not unusual to find women still selling home-brewed beers in the market places. These thick tawny brews or "porridge beers" are cheap and must be consumed within two or three days. They are generally regarded by African drinkers as more nutritious than pale European lagers.

Commercially brewed sorghum (millet) beers have been produced in South Africa from the early 20th century to meet the demand for beer from the black, urban population. They originated in Natal. Their popularity, however, is partly due to the fact that until 1962, the majority of the population was not allowed to buy European-style beers.

Although the consumption of golden lagers has certainly soared, sorghum beers remain popular and there has been no major switch to lagers.

abbey at Floreffe. The best, a mahogany-coloured spicy ale, is simply called La Meilleure (8%). A golden tripel (7.5%) is also sold as Abbaye de Bonne Espérance. Additional beers include a tasty dubbel and a blonde (both 7%).

FOSTER'S BEER (AUSTRALIA)

This light, fruity lager (4%) has a world-wide reputation and is the beer most drinkers abroad associate with Australia. Originally founded in Melbourne in 1888, Foster's was a lager pioneer, importing ice-making equipment from America. It was also a bottled beer specialist and leader in the export field.

FRAOCH (SCOTLAND)

Bruce Williams has been brewing Fraoch (the Gaelic word for "heather") at Maclay's Alloa brewery every flowering season since 1993. Instead of adding hops, which are not grown in Scotland, to the boiling wort, he follows the example of the ancient Picts and uses native heather tips and myrtle leaves. The hot liquid is also infused in a vat of fresh heather flowers before fermentation. The spicy, floral brew that results comes in two strengths, Heather Ale (4.1%) and Pictish Ale (5.4%).

GHILLIE, THE (SCOTLAND)

This distinctive bottled ale (4.5%) is produced by the Broughton brewery.

GOLD LABEL (ENGLAND)

England's best-known bottled barley wine. This spicy, warming brew (10.9%) is produced by Whitbread.

GOSSER (AUSTRIA)

The Gosser brewery produces a light lager, Gosser-Gold, the gold, malty Gosser Märzen, a fruity, malty Gosser Spezial and a sweet Gosser Export.

GOUDEN CAROLUS (BELGIUM)

This distinctive, smooth, dark ale (7%) is from the family-run Anker brewery of Mechelen. Its name derives from a gold coin that featured the Holy Roman Emperor Charles V who had grown up in the city. There is also a lighter, less spicy Mechelsen Brune (5.5%) and a yellow, pale ale, Toison d' Or Tripel (7%).

GROLSCH PILSNER (HOLLAND)

A fresh, hoppy Pilsner (5%), which is brewed using only malt, hops, yeast and water and left unpasteurized in the bottle, even in the export version. (The canned premium lager is pasteurized.) The large independent brewery is probably as well known for its distinctive, swing-stoppered bottles, which date from 1897, as it is for the contents.

GRØN (DENMARK)

Tuborg's main brand is known as Grøn, after the green colour of the label. There is a premium Guld (gold) and a dark lager Rod (red).

HSB (ENGLAND)

This famous, full-bodied bitter (4.8%) is produced by Gale's, which is a family brewery in Horndean, Hampshire.

HARP LAGER (IRELAND)

This pioneering golden lager (3.6%) was developed by Guinness in 1959 particularly to mark the bicentenary of the company. Harp was launched in 1960 and was named after the company's famous harp logo. It is brewed at the Great Northern Brewery in Dundalk.

☆ MY GOODNESS, MY GUINNESS ☆

Having set up his Dublin brewery in 1759, Arthur Guinness initially produced ale. Seeing the success of imported English porter, he changed direction and, by 1799, his complete output was porter. Single-handedly, he reversed the beer trade, sending exports to England. By 1815, Guinness was so well known that wounded officers at the Battle of Waterloo were calling for the beer by name.

The second Arthur Guinness perfected an extra stout porter during the 1820s and this eventually became known simply as stout. He made Guinness the largest brewer in Ireland. His son, Benjamin, turned St James's Gate into the largest

brewery in the world, its stout selling around the globe.

The label with its harp trademark first appeared in 1862. By around 1910,

Guinness was producing two million hogsheads, (245-litre/54-gallon casks) a year in a new brewery.

A second brewery was opened in London in 1936 to meet demand in England and since then, Guinness breweries have been built around the world. The stout is also brewed under licence in many countries, from North America to Australia.

In the 1950s, Guinness re-entered the ale trade with a beer called Phoenix and celebrated its bicentenary in 1959 by developing its own Harp lager. However, stout remains at the heart of the enterprise. A quality bottled stout, Guinness Extra Stout (4.3%), is undoubtedly one of the world's classic beers. It uses unmalted roasted barley and is heavily hopped with a ruby-black colour and a complex bitter flavour. It is unpasteurized in Ireland. Guinness Foreign Extra Stout (7.5%) is partly blended to create a richly astringent taste. Guinness Special Export (8%) is produced exclusively for the Belgian market.

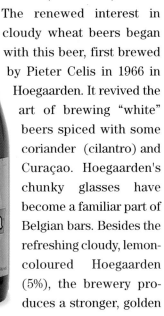

HOEGAARDEN (BELGIUM)

The renewed interest in cloudy wheat beers began with this beer, first brewed by Pieter Celis in 1966 in Hoegaarden. It revived the art of brewing "white" beers spiced with some coriander (cilantro) and Curaçao. Hoegaarden's chunky glasses have become a familiar part of Belgian bars. Besides the refreshing cloudy, lemon-coloured Hoegaarden (5%), the brewery produces a stronger, golden Grand Cru and a spicier orangey-coloured Julius (both (8.7%), plus a rich, fruity brown ale, Verboden Vrucht (8.8%). All are bottle-conditioned.

HOLSTEN PILS (GERMANY)

The widely available premium Pilsner (5%) from the Holsten brewery in Hamburg is one of a few in that firm's famous dry, hoppy range, which also includes the Edel Pilsner and Premium Bier.

IMPERIAL RUSSIAN STOUT (ENGLAND)

A classic beer from Scottish Courage, the vintage dark-brown, smooth brew (10%) has a rich malty flavour.

JACOBITE ALE (SCOTLAND)

This strong brew (8%) is fermented in oak and flavoured with coriander (cilantro). It is made by the Traquair House brewery at Innerleithen, near Peebles. A rare survivor from an age when great manor houses all had their own breweries, and dating from the 12th century, it is said to be the oldest inhabited building in Scotland. All the beer is fermented in oak vessels and also includes Bear

Ale (5%) and Traquair House Ale, a strong classic ale (7.2%) with a fruity, malt flavour and slight dryness.

JENLAIN (FRANCE)

This strong, reddish-amber, all-malt bière de garde (6.5%) is the best known of its type. It is a top-fermented brew, packed with spicy, fruity flavours. The Duyck brewery of Jenlain, near Valenciennes, still sells Jenlain in classic corked and wired bottles, but it is also available in smaller, capped bottles.

JEVER (GERMANY)

This is probably the most bitter beer produced in Germany. Jever Pilsner underlines the general German rule that beers become drier as you travel north. The brewery of the same name, dating back to 1848, is famed for its Pilsner (4.9%), which has a heady, hoppy aroma and an intense bitterness. Owned by Bavaria St Pauli of Hamburg since 1923, a modern brewery was built in 1992 in this old North Sea resort. Its other brews include Jever Light (2.7%) and the alcohol-free Jever Fun.

JOHN SMITH'S BITTER (ENGLAND)

This is a dark-amber, sweetish, malty cask bitter (3.8%) with a creamy texture, from Yorkshire. One of the most popular beers in England.

JUPILER (BELGIUM)

Belgium's best-selling beer, the popular malty Pilsner (5.2%) comes from Jupille near Liège. Founded in 1853, the brewery is now part of Interbrew.

KAISER (AUSTRIA)

Kaiser is Austria's leading beer brand. Besides a standard Kaiser draught (draft), the range also includes a malty vollbier called Kaiser Märzen (5.2%), a Spezial Kaiser Goldquell (5.6%), and a hoppier Pilsner called Kaiser Premium (5.4%). Other Kaiser beers include the dark Doppelmaltz (4.7%) and the stronger Kaiser Piccolo Bock (7.1%).

KILKENNY IRISH BEER (IRELAND)

This red ale (4.3%) is a creamy, premium ale, initially produced for export in 1987 by Smithwick's. It was launched in Ireland in 1995. A stronger version (5%) is exported to the United States.

KIRIN BEER (JAPAN)

Japan's best-selling beer (4.9%) is a crisp, full-bodied and fresh-flavoured Pilsner brewed using Saaz and Hallertau hops. It is matured for up to two months before being sold unpasteurized. Kirin's other main beer is Ichiban Shibori, a soft, golden lager (5.5%) and the company also brews a wide range of local and speciality beers.

KOFF PORTER (FINLAND)

The Sinebrychoff brewery still brews one of its oldest beers (7.2%), a dense dark ale which was only revived after World War II, using a top-fermenting yeast cultured from a bottle of Guinness. Centrifuged but not filtered, it has a rich, roasted flavour. Four different malts are used in the mash, and the beer is conditioned

for six weeks before it is pasteurized. It was once exported to the United States under the name Imperial Stout.

KRONENBOURG (FRANCE)

The main Kronenbourg beer (5.2%) is a light-tasting lager and the stronger 1664 (5.9%), popularly known as "soixante-quatre", is smoother but a little more full-bodied. There is also a weaker Kronenbourg Légère (3.1%). A hoppier variant of the standard lager is called Kronenbourg Tradition Allemande, while Kronenbourg Anglaise is softer and deeper amber in colour. There is also a maltier, dark version of 1664 called Brune, and two seasonal brews, a rosy La Bière de Noël and a golden Kronenbourg Bière de Mars.

KULMINATOR 28 (GERMANY)

One of the strongest beers in the world, the threateningly named Kulminator 28 has an alcohol content of more than 12%, the highest gravity of any bottom-fermenting beer. The brew is matured for nine months, including a short period of freezing, to produce this intensely malty, heavyweight, amber beer. There is a less threatening and darker conventional Kulminator Doppelbock (7.6%), without the number. Both of the beers are brewed by EKU in the Bavarian town of Kulmbach, and are widely exported.

LA TRAPPE (HOLLAND)

A range of four Trappist top-fermenting, bottle-conditioned ales from the Koningshoeven Trappist monastery. The beers rise in strength, starting from the pale-amber, fresh, fruity enkel (5.5%). Enkel is one the few "single" strength Trappist ales brewed for the monks' everyday consumption that is available commercially. The dark, deep-red, dry dubbel (6.5%) is the next strongest brew, followed by a paler and more bronze-coloured, spicier tripel (8%). The rich, reddish-coloured, vintage, heavyweight brew quadrupel (10%) makes an ideal nightcap for the dedicated beer drinker.

LION LAGER (SOUTH AFRICA)

Together with Castle, this is a leading lager (5%) from South African Breweries. It is slightly sweeter than Castle. The Lion brand has been roaring since a Norwegian merchant Anders Ohlsson, who had been involved in beer brewing in Africa since 1862, established the Annaberg brewery in Cape Town in 1883.

LONDON PRIDE (ENGLAND)

Fuller's fine, deep-red best bitter (4.1%) has a rich, dry, malty, hoppy taste.

LÖWENBRÄU PREMIUM PILS (GERMANY)

This light, refreshing, golden lager is made in Munich according to the Bavarian purity law, with Hallertau hops, spring barley and yeast.

MACKESON'S STOUT (ENGLAND)

This best-known bottled sweet stout (3%) from Whitbread is a blackish colour with a sugary, fruity taste. When it was first brewed, in 1907, it was claimed to be a

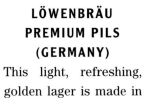

☆ ICE BEER ☆

As the alcohol content rises in a brew, the action of the yeast is subdued, making fermentation difficult. If the brew is frozen, the water freezes before the alcohol and can be removed to make a concentrated beer.

However, it is the beer's lack of flavour that has become popular. Few of the ultra-smooth lagers weigh in at more than 5.5%, although Tennent's of Scotland produced a Super Ice at 8.6%.

Many ice beers were originally developed in Canada by Labatt in 1993, and they are now produced by major brewers in the United States and Australia.

tonic for invalids because it contained milk sugar, or lactose. The sugar does not ferment, so the beer is low in alcohol. Mackeson's was called milk stout until the British Government banned the term in 1946. However, Whitbread continues the connection by depicting a milk churn on the label. It is still the leading brand in a declining sweet stout market.

LABATT ICE BEER (CANADA)

This pioneering ice beer, with a golden colour and full body, weighs in at 5.6%. Labatt's Blue (5%) is in fact the brewery's main lager.

LEFFE (BELGIUM)

Interbrew produces this range of abbey beers, named after the Leffe abbey. There is an amber-coloured blonde and a dark-brown, malty, fruity brune (both 6.5%), a golden tripel (8.4%) and two brown ales, Vieille Cuvée (7.8%) and Radieuse (8.2%).

MANN'S ORIGINAL (ENGLAND)

England's best-known bottled, sweet brown ale (2.8%) has a sticky, sugary texture and a fruity taste, and is now brewed by Ushers in Wiltshire.

McEWAN'S EXPORT (SCOTLAND)

A sweet and malty Scottish ale (4.5%) produced by McEwan's in Edinburgh.

MOLSON CANADIAN LAGER (CANADA)

The most famous of Molson's products (5%) is pale gold with a dry malt nose and hints of hops. Its flavour is smooth and well-balanced. The oldest brewery in North America and a rival to Labatt, Molson also produces Special Dry lager (5.5%) as well as a new range of malt beers.

MOOSEHEAD LAGER (CANADA)

This is the popular, mild pale-malt lager (5%) that gave its name to the oldest independent brewery in Canada, founded in 1867. The company also produces local Alpine Lager (5%) for the Maritime Provinces, and a dry Moosehead Pale Ale.

MURPHY'S IRISH STOUT (IRELAND)

This relatively light, smooth stout (4%) should be served cooled to lager temperature, with a head about 1½cm (½in) deep. Established in 1856, today Murphy's Stout is exported to more than 50 countries.

WHAT'S IN ☆ A NAME? ☆

Budweiser Budvar (5%), the internationally renowned all-malt lager from the Czech Republic, is perhaps now the classic example of its style. The company was founded in the town of Ceské Budejovice (Budweis in German) in 1895, and rapidly became a major exporter and successful company.

Such is the fame of Budweiser Budvar, that many leading breweries around the world have proposed mergers, but none so persistently as Anheuser-Busch of the United States, which sells its own leading beer under the Budweiser name. The American lager – and the world's leading beer brand – is very different, with a crisp, clean taste that belies its alcohol content of 4.7%. The companies have often clashed in the courts over the rights to the famous title.

NASTRO AZZURO (ITALY)

Peroni's pale-gold, clean, sweetish premium Pilsner (5.2%) was introduced in 1964. The name means "Blue Ribbon". The brewery also produces a lighter Peroni Birra, similar regional brands and a more full-bodied bottled Gran Riserva in 1996.

NEGRA MODELO (MEXICO)

Despite its name, Negra Modelo (Black Model) (5.3%) is more of a deep amber-brown colour. It is a cross between a spicy Vienna red and a softer Munich dunkel, with a chocolate aroma, a hint of fruit and spices, and a hop finish. This classic beer enjoys a justified international reputation.

NEWCASTLE BROWN ALE (ENGLAND)

This pioneering northern brown ale (4.7%) has a nutty, caramel taste. It was first produced by Newcastle Breweries in 1927. Newcastle Brown is strong, dry and light in colour. Drinkers can expect a small glass, so they can keep topping up. This best-selling bottled beer is exported to more than 40 countries. It is brewed by Scottish Courage in Tyneside, Scotland.

OLD PECULIER (ENGLAND)

Theakston's famous, rich, dark old ale (5.7%) with a roast-malt flavour, comes from Masham, North Yorkshire. The odd name refers to the Peculier of Masham, the town's ancient ecclesiastical court. The company is owned by Scottish Courage.

OLD SPECKLED HEN (ENGLAND)

A deep-gold, premium pale ale (5.2%) with a good malt, hop balance from Morland's of Abingdon, Oxfordshire. It is not named after a farmyard fowl but an old MG car made in the town, which was speckled black and gold.

ORIGINAL PORTER (ENGLAND)

A ruby-brown porter with a roast-malt and liquorice flavour, which is created from the liquorice that is actually used in the recipe (5.2%). This is produced by the Shepherd Neame brewery, Kent.

ORVAL (BELGIUM)

This classic Trappist ale (6.2%) is the only brew made by the Abbaye d'Orval. It is orange, with a heady, hoppy aroma and an intense, dry flavour. Its complex character is in part due to three separate fermentations and dry-hopping.

PALM (BELGIUM)

Palm Spéciale (5.2%) is the biggest-selling ale in Belgium. It is brewed by the independent Palm brewery of Steenhuffel. It is an amber, fruity, refreshing beer. A darker version called Dobbel Palm (5.5%) is specially produced at Christmas. The village brewery, which dates back to 1747, also brews a more powerful and copper-coloured, bottle-conditioned ale called Aerts 1900 (7%), as well as a wheat beer, Steendonk (4.5%).

PEDIGREE (ENGLAND)

A classic, coppery coloured pale ale (4.5%) with a dry hop and malt taste and spicy overtones, from Marston's of Burton-on-Trent. It is brewed by the Burton Union system.

PETE'S WICKED WINTER BREW (UNITED STATES)

This delicious, red-amber ale (4.2%) has hints of nutmeg and raspberry in its fruity flavour. It is one of many in the wide range of speciality brews from Pete's Brewing Company.

PILSNER URQUELL (CZECH REPUBLIC)

The original flagship Pilsner of the Czech brewing industry. Its development in Plzen launched golden lager on the world for the first time in 1842. Pilsner Urquell (4.4%) is still a quality beer by any standards, particularly when fresh, with its delicate hop aroma and deep, soft fruitiness. The word Urquell means "original source".

PRIPPS BLA (SWEDEN)

This is the best-selling Swedish beer in all three strength classes. It is a honey-gold sweetish Pilsner. There is also a new Extra Strong Pripps Bla (7.2%) that is in the strongest beer class.

PYRAMID APRICOT ALE (UNITED STATES)

This mild ale (3.5%) has a subtle apricot taste from start to finish. One of the success stories of the craft brewery movement, the Pyramid brewery was set up as Hart Brewing in 1984 in the small logging town of Kalama in Washington State, brewing a Pyramid Pale Ale. Since then, Pyramid has now grown into the third-largest of new ventures to be found within the United States. The group of Pyramid ales include Pyramid Pale Ale, Pyramid Wheaten Ale, Pyramid Best Brown and Pyramid Rye (all 5.1%). The company also brews a range of seasonal brews that includes Porter (5.4%) and Snow Cap (6.9%).

RAM ROD (ENGLAND)

A full-bodied ale (5%) with a bitter hops and malt flavour, produced by Young's brewery in Wandsworth, London. This firmly traditional family brewery is noted for its cask beers. Local deliveries are still made by horse-drawn drays and the Victorian Ram Brewery houses geese, peacocks and a ram (the company mascot). In recent years, Young's has added seasonal ales to its output, including a wheat beer.

RED ERIK (DENMARK)

This lager from Ceres is named in honour of the Viking who discovered Greenland and then began brewing there. The brewery he founded, named after the goddess of grain, is now part of the second

☆ OKTOBERFEST ☆

Mention Germany and beer, and many people envisage Munich's famous Oktoberfest, when in 16 days (at the end of September), around 6 million litres (1,319,814 gallons) of beer will be drunk in huge canvas beer halls by thousands of visitors. It is the world's biggest beer festival.

This mad annual party began when the Bavarian Prince Ludwig married Princess Theresa in 1810 and the city threw a huge celebration. It was such a success that it has been repeated ever since. Only the six major breweries in Munich are allowed to supply beer. In 1882, Spaten created the amber-coloured Oktoberfest beer that has been served ever since.

largest brewing group in all of Denmark. Besides a range of Pilsners, it brews a strong dark Ceres Stowt (stout, 7.7%) and a range of stronger golden lagers that are widely exported.

RED HOOK ESB (UNITED STATES)

This deep-amber, strong extra-special bitter (5.4%) comes from the ground-breaking Red Hook brewery, founded in 1981 by Paul Shipman and Gordon Bowker in the Ballard area of Seattle, Washington. The brewery also produces Red Hook Rye, a golden, unfiltered beer (5%) with a dry, grainy flavour. Red Hook has recently embarked on a series of developments and expansions, and it is rapidly becoming an established national brewer.

RED STRIPE (JAMAICA)

This pale-gold, lightly hopped lager (4.7%) with a full flavour, is from the family-run Desnoes & Geddes in Kingston, Jamaica. It is now produced under licence in the United Kingdom, where it is a strong favourite with the West Indian population.

RINGNES PILS (NORWAY)

A golden Pilsner-style lager with a fresh, mild hop and malt flavour. This is the flagship brand for Ringnes, Norway's major brewery, founded in 1877.

ROLLING ROCK (UNITED STATES)

This lager brand revived the fortunes of the Latrobe brewery of Pennsylvania, founded in 1893. The light lager stands out from the crowd due to the fired-on label on its green bottles.

ROSE DE GAMBRINUS (BELGIUM)

The most celebrated lambic frambozen (5%), which comes from the Cantillon brewery in Brussels. It contains a small proportion of cherries and a dash of vanilla, as well as raspberries. It is blood-orange coloured, and tastes fruity.

ROSSA (ITALY)

This is probably the most characterful of Italy's red beers. The rosy-amber and richly flavoured, all-malt, La Rossa (7.5%), from Moretti of Udine, gives a robust reminder of northern Italy's former connections with Vienna and its range of Märzen-style brews.

RUDDLES BEST BITTER (ENGLAND)

A characterful cask bitter (3.7%) originally from a famous Rutland brewery, it is now brewed by Morland's of Abingdon. It also produces Ruddles County, a full-bodied, malty cask bitter (4.9%).

SAGRES (PORTUGAL)

Central's best-selling fruity lager (5.1%) is sold in both popular, pale-yellow blonde (Sagres Pale) and rarer brown versions. The smoother, chocolatey, molasses-flavoured, dark brown beer is in the style of a Munich Dunkel. There is also a premium Sagres Golden.

SAHTI (FINLAND)

This is the traditional beer style of Finland. It is strong (usually around 8%), unfiltered, hazy, reddish-amber in colour and quite flat, with a spicy, bittersweet flavour. Rye, rather than barley, is used as the main component in the mash. This, combined with the main seasoning of juniper (rather than hops), gives the finished product a refreshingly tart tang. Juniper twigs are also used to strain the brew, and saunas are sometimes used to kiln the grains. Sahti production was originally a domestic enterprise, and baking yeast is often used in the recipe, reflecting its homely origins.

SALVATOR (GERMANY)

The pioneer of the doppelbock style from the famous Paulaner brewery. This rich, ruby brew (7.5%) is overpowering with its fruit-cake aroma and warming flavour.

SAMICHLAUS (SWITZERLAND)

Classed as the world's strongest lager at a staggering 14%, Samichlaus (Santa Claus) is brewed just once a year at the beginning of December by Hürlimann of Zurich and is then left to mature for 12 months before being ready to redden Father Christmas's nose the following festive season. This reddish-brown brew, first introduced in 1980, is testimony to the gutsy fighting qualities of Hürlimann's quality yeast strain, and a constant contender for the *Guinness Book of Records*. With its highly alcoholic cognac and cough-mixture character, it is a smooth beer to sip and savour before going to sleep.

SAMUEL ADAMS BOSTON LAGER (UNITED STATES)

This bright-amber Pilsner has a fresh, hoppy nose, a sweet-malt entry, a caramel flavour and a dry, malty finish. It is brewed by the Boston Beer Company and the range of brews is named after one of the organizers of the Boston Tea Party of 1773. The company also produces Samuel Adams Boston Stock Ale, a bright-amber ale (5%) with a complex, earthy nose and a hoppy, off-dry palate.

✫ EASTERN EUROPE ✫

Some former Communist countries of Eastern Europe, namely Hungary, Bulgaria, Romania, Latvia, Lithuania and Estonia, consume relatively little beer, in part due to a strong spirit-imbibing or wine-drinking tradition, but also because of inadequate brewing capacity and a shortage of raw materials. However, Hungary, Bulgaria and Romania have a healthy appetite for light lagers. Aldaris, a yeasty lager, is the biggest brewer in Latvia.

Foreign companies have shown great interest in the region since the move away from Communism and many countries have welcomed their investment. Hungary's brewing industry is now almost entirely foreign-owned and overseas investors have an interest in more than a third of Bulgaria's 13 breweries. Since 1991, a joint

company called Baltic Beverages Holding (BBH), established by Scandinavian brewers, has taken a major stake in the leading breweries of Estonia, Latvia and Lithuania. They have now been modernized and the beer ranges revamped to a more international style of Pilsners, moving away from traditional beers.

Russia and the Ukraine were once producing a range of German, Czech and even English-style beers, but the Revolution and two world wars severely damaged the brewing industry. Later, Gorbachev's drive against alcohol meant that some recovering breweries were either mothballed or turned into soft drinks factories. Foreign investment has not been welcomed, although imports, especially from the Czech Republic, are increasing. Local beers include the home-made rye brew, Kvass.

BREWING IN THE ☆ PACIFIC ☆

Throughout the hundreds of Pacific islands, breweries are gallantly turning out brews for the small populations, such as Vailima from New Zealand. In the 1940s, Australians, working in the gold fields of Papua New Guinea, frustrated by the lack of good quality beer, built their own brewery in Port Morseby and used rainwater collected in tanks as liquor. Production started in 1952 and sales soared in the 1960s when Prohibition ended.

The South Pacific brewery now produces a range of lagers, and its South Pacific Export (5.5%) won the Brewex international gold medal award in 1980. Similarly, the Brasserie de Tahiti won a World Gold Medal in 1990 for its prestigious pale gold Hinano Tahiti lager (4.9%).

SAMUEL SMITH'S PALE ALE (ENGLAND)

This distinctive orangey-coloured bottled pale ale (5%) is brewed by the fiercely independent Samuel Smith family brewery in Tadcaster. Beer is still fermented in Yorkshire slate squares and racked in wooden casks there. Other fine brews include Old Brewery Bitter, a nutty cask bitter (4%), Samuel Smith's Imperial Stout, a rich, heavy, bottled stout (7%), which is best served and enjoyed as a liqueur, and Taddy Porter, a distinctive, dark brown, rich, dry, bottled porter (5%).

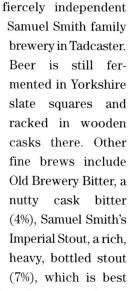

SAN MIGUEL PREMIUM (SPAIN)

The malty, hoppy flagship lager of the San Miguel company is a relatively strong lager (5.4%) with light, citrus notes and good body. Like much of the company's output, it is aimed at the quality end of the market.

SAPPORO ORIGINAL DRAFT BLACK LABEL (JAPAN)

The fourth best-selling beer in Japan, this lively, light Pilsner (4.7%) was the first to use the micro-filtration technique instead of pasteurization to produce what is called a "draft" beer. It is sold abroad in stylish silver cans as Sapporo Draft.

SCHIEHALLION LAGER (SCOTLAND)

A cask-conditioned, Bohemian-style lager (4.8%), brewed using German Hersbrucker hops, from the Harviestoun brewery. It won a Gold Medal at the Great British Beer Festival in 1996. Schiehallion is a local mountain, which was once climbed by Astronomer Royal Nevil Maskelyne.

SCHNEIDER WEISSE (GERMANY)

A refreshing, yeasty wheat beer (5.4%) brewed by the Schneider brewery. This is the classic example of the Weisse style. Besides the Original Hefeweizenbier, the Bavarian brewery also produces a filtered Kristall, a weaker Weizen-hell (4.9%) and a light beer (2.9%).

SHEAF STOUT (AUSTRALIA)

This dry, bitter, top-fermented stout (5.7%) from Tooth's brewery in Sydney, which was founded in 1835, is one of Australia's most distinctive-tasting beers.

SIERRA NEVADA CELEBRATION ALE (UNITED STATES)

This is one of the best of the American IPAs. It is a copper-coloured ale (5.1%), brewed by Sierra Nevada Brewing. It has a pungent, floral nose with hints of caramel malt and a roasted malt and earthy hops flavour with a long, full-bodied finish.

SIMBA LAGER (ZAIRE)

A popular golden lager in Zaire, formerly the Belgian Congo, Simba has been produced by the Brasimba brewery in which the Belgian giant Interbrew has a stake.

SINGHA (THAILAND)

A bright gold lager (6%) with a hoppy flavour, brewed by the Boon Rawd Brewery. It is named after the mythical half-lion creature shown on the label. The brewery was set up in Bangkok in the 19th century, using German technology.

SMITHWICK'S BARLEY WINE (IRELAND)

Despite its name, this barley wine (5.5%) is brewed at Macardle's brewery in Dundalk.

SOL (MEXICO)

In the 1980s, the Moctezuma brewery's Sol succeeded Corona Extra as the fashionable Mexican beer to drink. Sol (4.6%) is a thin, light lager with a high proportion of adjuncts. Like its arch-rival, it is sold in a distinctive, embossed bottle.

SPATEN UR-MÄRZEN (GERMANY)

This classic, full-bodied brew (5.6%) is produced by Spaten, the Munich brewery that was at the heart of the bottom-fermenting lager revolution of the 19th century. The company is still justly proud of its lagers, notably its malty Münchner Hell (4.8%) and dunkel (5%). The company also brews a dry Pilsner (5%) and a golden maibock (6.5%), as well as a stronger doppelbock, Optimator (6.8%).

introduced as Steinecker in 1958, named after the new, German-made, Steinecker continuous-fermentation brewing plant that had been installed in its Auckland brewery. After a legal challenge in the United States from Dutch giant Heineken, the name was then changed to Steinlager in 1962.

STELLA ARTOIS (BELGIUM)

Belgium's best-known, golden lager is the flagship Pilsner (5.2%) produced by the brewing giant, Interbrew.

SUPER BOCK (PORTUGAL)

Unicer's pale, robust, malty, fruity lager (5.8%) is one of the most popular brands drunk in Portugal.

SWAN DRAUGHT (AUSTRALIA)

This crisp, gold, malty lager (4.9%) is the best-known beer produced by the Swan plant. Others include Swan Export lager and Swan Gold (3.5%).

SPENDRUP'S PREMIUM (SWEDEN)

This flavoursome, full-bodied, all-malt premium Pilsner comes from the Spendrup's brewery in Grangesberg.

STAROPRAMEN (CZECH REPUBLIC)

Besides a fresh and hoppy pale 10 (4.2%), this major Prague brewery produces a full-bodied 12 (4.6%). The quality of the beers reflects the fact that the brewery has retained traditional methods of brewing.

STEINLAGER (NEW ZEALAND)

Lion's premium, pale-gold, international lager (5%), much drier and more aromatic than its other beers, is mainly sold abroad. This sweetish, hoppy brew was originally

TECATE (MEXICO)

Launched in the 1950s by Cuauhtémoc of Mexico, this pale, light ("clara") lager (4.5%) is low in flavour, but good for satisfying thirst in a hot climate. It was originally served with salt and fresh lemons, which may have inspired the more recent craze for drinking Mexican lagers with a slice of lime.

TENNENT'S LAGER (SCOTLAND)

This fizzy, golden keg lager (4%) is the mainstay of the Tennent's brewery's lager range, which includes a grainy, pale-gold Pilsner (3.4%), a stronger Extra (4.8%), Gold (5%) and a weighty, amber-coloured, sweetish, strong Super (9%). Tennent's are Scotland's dominant lager brewers.

TETLEY BITTER (ENGLAND)

This pale-amber, hoppy, fruity bitter (3.7%) is traditionally served through a tight tap to give a creamy head. It is brewed by Tetley in Leeds, which after a merger in 1993 is now called Carlsberg-Tetley.

THEAKSTON BEST BITTER (ENGLAND)

A bright-gold, soft bitter (3.8%) with a nutty flavour, which originally came from the North Yorkshire Theakston brewery in Masham. It is now also brewed by Scottish Courage in Newcastle.

THOMAS HARDY'S ALE (ENGLAND)

This bottle-conditioned ale (12%) was introduced by Eldridge Pope of Dorset in 1968 to celebrate that summer's Thomas Hardy festival in Dorchester, marking the 40th anniversary of the novelist's death. It was brewed the previous autumn "about as strong as it is possible to brew" by head brewer Denis Holliday to match Hardy's description of Dorchester strong ale in his novel *The Trumpet Major*: "It was of the most beautiful colour that the eye of an artist in beer could desire; full in body yet brisk as a volcano; piquant, yet without a twang; luminous as an autumn sunset; free from streakiness of taste; but, finally, rather heady." After maturing in casks for six months, the highly hopped ale was filled into bottles, corked, sealed with wax and displayed with velvet ribbons. It was expected to be a one-off special brew, but such was demand that it was repeated, and now drinkers compare different vintages. Each bottle is year-dated and matures gradually from a rich, fruity brew when young to a deeper, mellower flavour.

☆ 74 YEARS OF PROHIBITION ☆

During World War I, the governments of many countries took action to restrict or ban drinking intoxicants. Britain slashed the number of hours that pubs could remain open. Many Canadian states introduced Prohibition, which became national in 1918, and Finland applied Prohibition from the start of the war. The most famous or notorious instance was later in the United States, with the Volstead Act of 1920.

However, the small northerly island of Iceland was even more assiduous in protecting its citizens from the demon drink, in spite of its Viking heritage. Prohibition came into effect in 1915 and the ban did not end until 1989. Until then, companies, such as the family-run Egill brewery of Reykjavík, could produce only soft drinks and low-alcohol beers. Stronger brews have now appeared, such as Gull, a golden, Pilsner export lager (5%). Reykjavík is fast gaining a reputation for being a fun-loving town, although alcoholism is a growing social problem there.

TOOHEYS OLD BLACK (AUSTRALIA)

A dark, fruity ale (4.4%) from Tooheys brewery. It is one of the few surviving "Old" top-fermenting beers produced by this concern.

TSINGTAO BEER (CHINA)

A pale-gold, Pilsner-style lager (5%), with a malt and hops, vanilla flavour, brewed by the Tsingtao brewery in Quingdao, Shandong province. Tsingtao is widely exported around the world in bottles and cans, partly to fuel the thirst of Chinese

populations in other countries. It is also popular among Westerners as an accompaniment to Chinese food. There is also a deep-amber Tsingtao Dark Beer.

TUSKER (KENYA)

Kenya Breweries' creamy, dry, golden lager appears in a variety of strengths. Tusker Premium, a strong, all-malt beer (5%), is brewed for international export. According to legend, it was named after the angry elephant which trampled to death one of the two founding brothers.

VICTORIA BEER (AUSTRALIA)

Despite the international reputation of Foster's Lager, this is the best-selling beer in Australia (4.9%). It accounts for a quarter of the total beer market and 60% of CUB's output. Melbourne Bitter is a similar beer.

VIEILLE PROVISION (BELGIUM)

An excellent, hoppy, saison-style ale (6.5%), which comes from the farmyard Dupont brewery. It is also known as Saison Dupont and Vieille Réserve. This classic country beer has a complex, refreshing taste and a solid creamy head.

WADWORTH 6X (ENGLAND)

Wadworth's premium fruity bitter (4.3%) from Devizes in Wiltshire has become well known beyond the south-west of England. It is also sold in bottles in a stronger version which clocks in at 5%.

WORTHINGTON'S WHITE SHIELD (ENGLAND)

This bottle-conditioned, pale ale (5.6%) has a delicate, yeasty, hoppy, malt flavour. It is now brewed by King and Barnes in Sussex. For years White Shield was the only widely available bottled pale ale that retained a sediment of yeast. This meant it was a living beer – a brewery in a bottle. Bar staff had to pour the ale steadily into the glass without disturbing the sediment, but some drinkers preferred their glass cloudy and added the yeast. It was not just a beer but a ritual.

XINGU (BRAZIL)

This Brazilian black beer (5%) is a modern version of the historic Amazonian drink. It is brewed by Cervejaría Cacador, using hops

rather than the original lupins to add flavour and act as a preservative. Sweet and malty, Xingu, named after a tributary of the Amazon River, is the fourth best-selling beer in South America.

YOUNGER'S TARTAN (SCOTLAND)

A dark-amber Scottish keg ale (3.7%) with a sweet and fruity flavour from William Younger of Edinburgh.

XXXB ALE (ENGLAND)

A complex-tasting premium bitter (4.8%) from Batemans of Lincolnshire.

Z (JAPAN)

Asahi brews this faintly fruity, top-fermenting light ale. The company claims that this unpasteurized brew is one of the "most technologically advanced beers" in Japan. Z beer is marketed specifically as a holiday drink.

"33" (FRANCE)

"Trente-trois" is quite a popular number in France, south-east Asia and Africa, where this light export Pilsner (4.8%) with a malted cereal flavour has developed a large market and following within the regions of the old French empire. It was originally brewed near Paris, but it is now produced in Marseilles.

Index